PANZER OPERATIONS

Germany's Panzer Group 3 during
the Invasion of Russia, 1941

HERMANN HOTH

Translated by Linden Lyons

CASEMATE
Philadelphia & Oxford

AN AUSA BOOK

Published in the United States of America and Great Britain in 2015 by
CASEMATE PUBLISHERS
1950 Lawrence Road, Havertown, PA 19083, USA
and
The Old Music Hall, 106–108 Cowley Road, Oxford OX4 1JE, UK

This edition © 2015 Association of the U.S. Army

Reprinted in paperback in 2017

Paperback edition: ISBN 978-1-61200-562-1

Cataloging-in-publication data is available from the Library of Congress and
the British Library.

Printed and bound in the United States of America

For a complete list of Casemate titles, please contact:

CASEMATE PUBLISHERS (US)
Telephone (610) 853-9131
Fax (610) 853-9146
Email: casemate@casematepublishers.com
www.casematepublishers.com

CASEMATE PUBLISHERS (UK)
Telephone (01865) 241249
Email: casemate-uk@casematepublishers.co.uk
www.casematepublishers.co.uk

FOREWORD TO THE 2017 EDITION

The history of the Second World War, and in particular the events that took place on the Eastern Front, continue to attract our interest and to capture our imagination over 70 years since its conclusion.

A plethora of literature has been published in the English language on this, the most devastating conflict the world has seen to this day. So, why do we need another book?

Panzer Operations was written by Hermann Hoth, arguably one of the most successful German military commanders of the Second World War. The book provides an insight into the mind of the general, and sheds light on the conduct of German armoured warfare in the summer of 1941. Too often, the early weeks and months of the war on the Eastern Front stand in the shadow of later events, such as the battles of Moscow, Stalingrad and Kursk. However, Operation *Barbarossa*, as the Germans codenamed their invasion of the Soviet Union, deserves to be studied in depth. German tactical superiority achieved some impressive operational goals, but, in the end, the Germans failed to achieve strategic victory.

There are some facts that need to be borne in mind when reading this book: Hoth wrote his piece in the 1950s—it was first published in German in 1956. At the time, accounts of the German experience of fighting the Soviets were in high demand, due to the onset of the Cold War. Hoth did not have all the sources available that the historian can use today—a large number of sources were still in the hands of the Allies who had captured the German archives in the final stages of the Second World War. Hoth also adopted a general approach that was common amongst German military writers at the time: they argued that German military excellence had been undermined by Hitler and his interference in the military conduct of operations. It was thus easy to blame the former Führer for the military defeat in the Second World War. Hoth is less outspoken about this in his writing than many other generals, but it is an underlying theme throughout the book. The truth, however, was far from black and white. The generals, including Hoth, had followed Hitler's orders for far too long, often against their better judgement and their knowledge of the tactical and operational situations at the front.

When read with these restrictions in mind, *Panzer Operations* is a fascinating read for everybody interested in the military history of the 20th century. "Papa" Hoth, as he was affectionately called by his soldiers, provides his personal account and view of Operation *Barbarossa*, and it is these first-hand insights that make this book so readable and important.

Dr Matthias Strohn, M.St., FRHistS
Visiting Fellow, Centre for Historical Analysis and Conflict Research
Senior Lecturer, Royal Military Academy Sandhurst
Senior Research Fellow, Buckingham University

CONTENTS

Dedicated to the memory of
General Walther von Hünersdorff

1941: Chief of the General Staff of Panzer Group 3
1943: killed in action as the commander of the 6th Panzer Division

PREFACE

....

This book does not purport to be a definitive account of the
military history of the Russian campaign, for there were too
few documents of any value. Official information from the Russian side
is unavailable. Unfortunately, surviving German war records remain
inaccessible for private research. This work is based on a privately held
copy of the 'Combat report of Panzer Group 3 in Russia, 10 February
1942', prepared in the field by the First General Staff Officer of Panzer
Group 3, Major Carl Wagener. This report contains not only valuable
map records from which the course of operations can be traced, but also
details on the considerations of the staff of the panzer group. It lacks
almost all of the intelligence reports on the enemy, the wording of the
orders received and adopted by the panzer group, and the reports by
the subordinate corps headquarters. These gaps could only be inadequately filled by some documents presented by the American prosecution during the High Command Trial in Nuremberg in 1948.

Nevertheless, there are two reasons for attempting a critical analysis
of the operations of a German armoured formation at the beginning of
the Russian campaign. First, it will be beneficial for future research on
military science to understand the motives which guided the actions of
Panzer Group 3. Second, some inaccuracies in previous publications
are corrected. Above all, though, this work should serve an educational
purpose. It aims to give practical examples of the operational use of armoured formations and thereby to contribute to the training of future
tank commanders.

In the first few months of the Russian campaign, Panzer Group 3 was the middlemost of the three northern German panzer groups. At the beginning of the campaign all three panzer groups were the principal means for executing the operational plan of the High Command. It is therefore natural to regard the operations of Panzer Group 3 not in isolation but in the context of the overall operations. For this purpose there are several documents available which were prepared for the Nuremberg Trials. Some of this material is still unpublished and unevaluated. They shed new light on the difficulties confronted by the military leadership. Even so, no final conclusions from the perspective of military history can be expected, because these documents represent only a selection, not the whole. Nonetheless, they are valuable for instructional purposes.

Given the instructional focus of this book, the performance of the troops and of the outstanding commanders is understated. The author hopes that the attentive reader will recognise how all the efforts of the leadership would have failed without the selfless dedication of the German soldier in battle against an enemy and country so alien and hostile in nature.

The author is indebted to the Institute of International Law at the University of Göttingen, and especially to Dr. Seraphim, for help in finding documentary evidence. The author is also grateful to retired Generals Otto von Knobelsdorff, Carl Wagener, and Joachim von Schön-Angerer for the use of material in their possession which relates to their part in the operations. Likewise, thanks to the retired Generals Friedrich Fangohr (†) and Ernst von Leyser for the information they provided.

Hoth
Goslar, summer 1956

MAPS

....

In view of the fact that Hermann Hoth describes the actions of Panzer Group 3 in detail in his text while referring readers to the specific corresponding maps, it has been decided to reproduce here the original postwar maps from his German edition.

At the end of the section the reader will find a list of place-names where the German spelling differs significantly from the English. In the meantime it may be useful to note that *Heeres-Gr. Nord* and *Heeres-Gr. Mitte* refer to Army Group North and Army Group Center, respectively. In regard to smaller units, taking the example on the lower half of Map 2, in the concentration around the city of Bialystok:

> *rd. 20 Schütz Div., 6 K.D., 2 Pz. Div, 6 mot Br.*
> translates to.
> approx. 20 Rifle (Infantry) Divisions, 6 Cavalry Divisions,
>   2 Tank Divisions, 6 Motorized Brigades

The German word *Feind* means enemy, or in this context, Soviet units. The word *Eisenbahnen* refers to railways. The map titles themselves are translated at the bottom of each page.

Linden Lyons

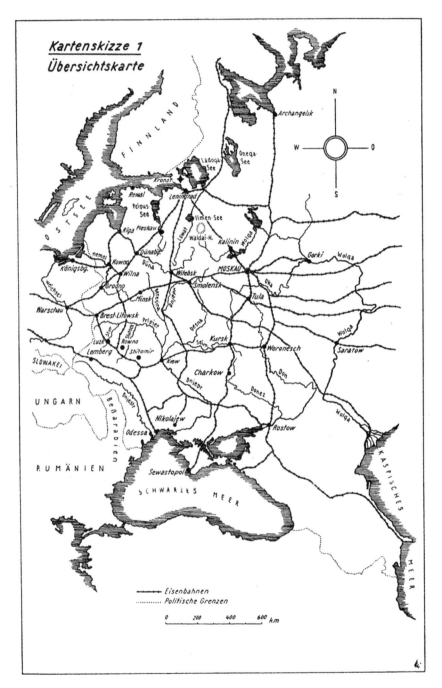

MAP 1: Overview

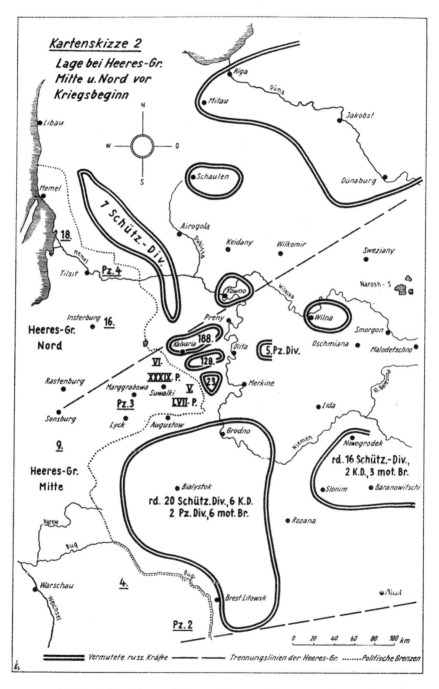

MAP 2: Position of Army Groups Centre and North
before the Invasion

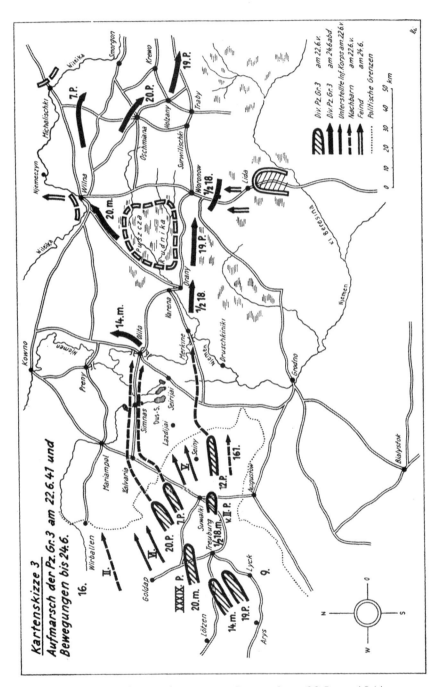

MAP 3: Advance by Panzer Group 3 on 22 June 1941
and movements until 24 June

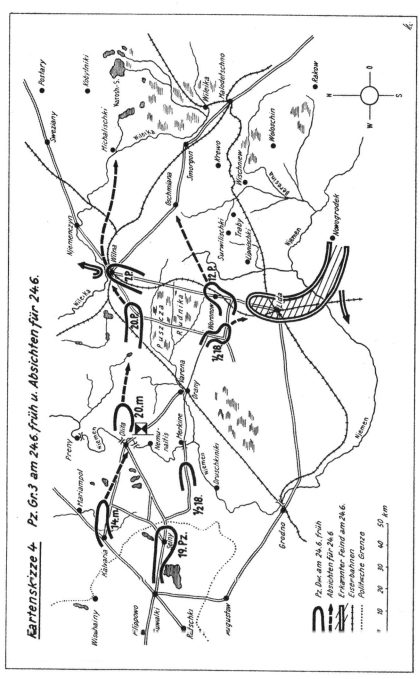

MAP 4: Panzer Group 3 at dawn on 24 June and
intentions for the day

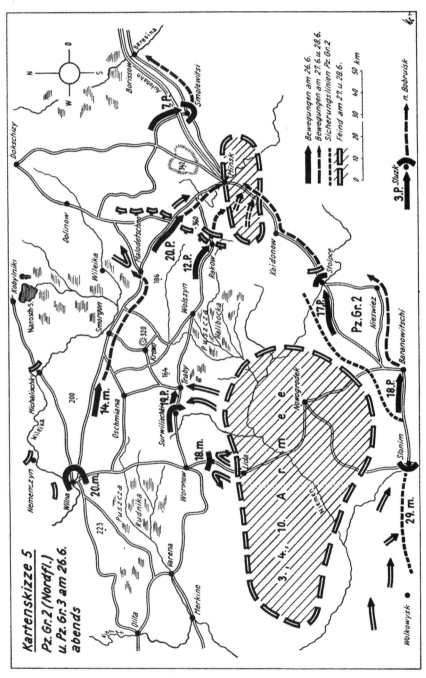

MAP 5: Panzer Group 2 (northern wing) and Panzer Group 3
on the evening of 26 June

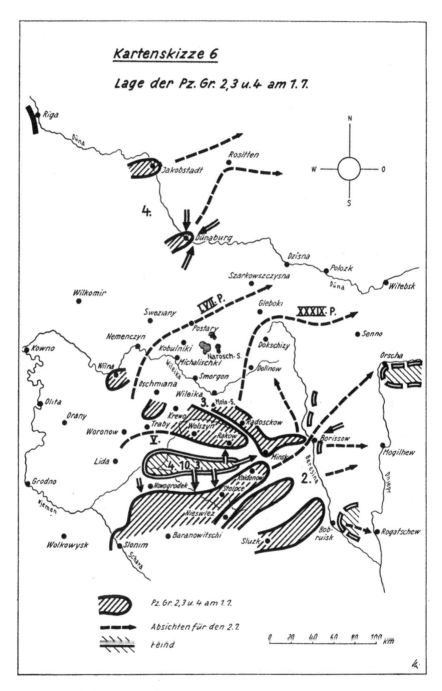

MAP 6: Position of Panzer Groups 2, 3 and 4 on 1 July 1941

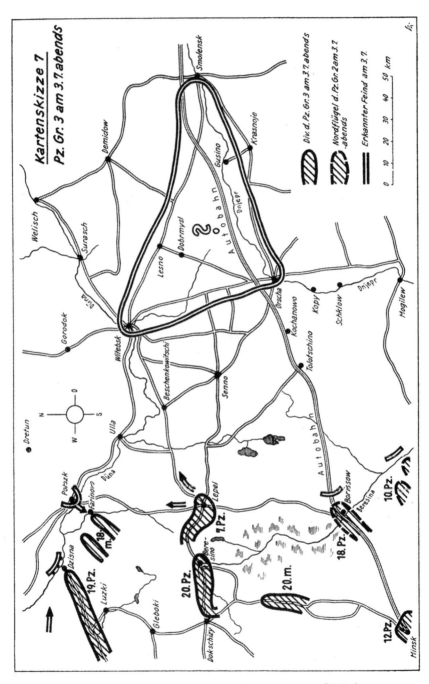

MAP 7: Panzer Group 3 on the evening of 3 July

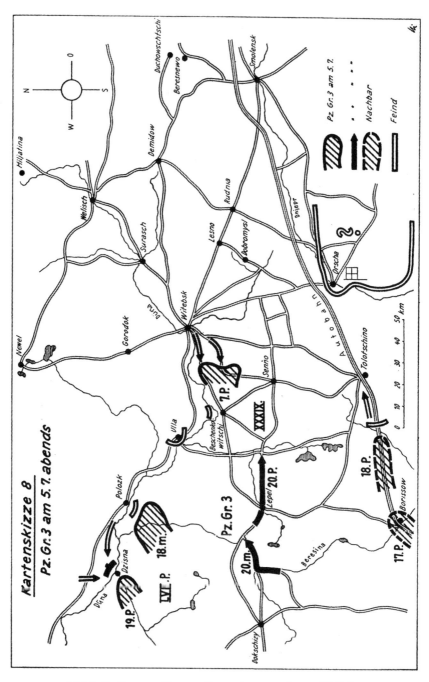

MAP 8: Panzer Group 3 on the evening of 5 July

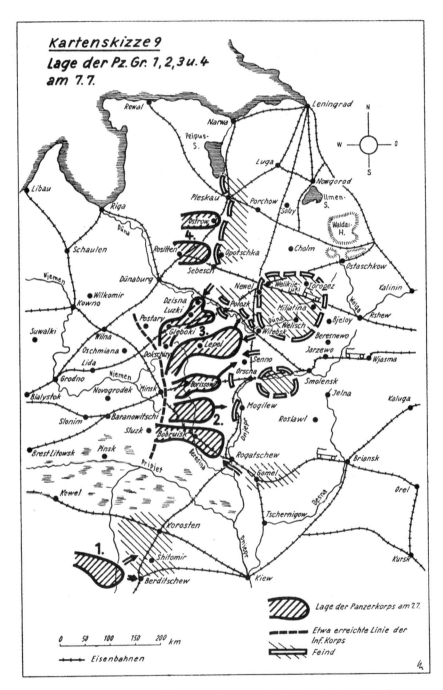

MAP 9: Position of Panzer Groups 1, 2, 3, and 4 on 7 July

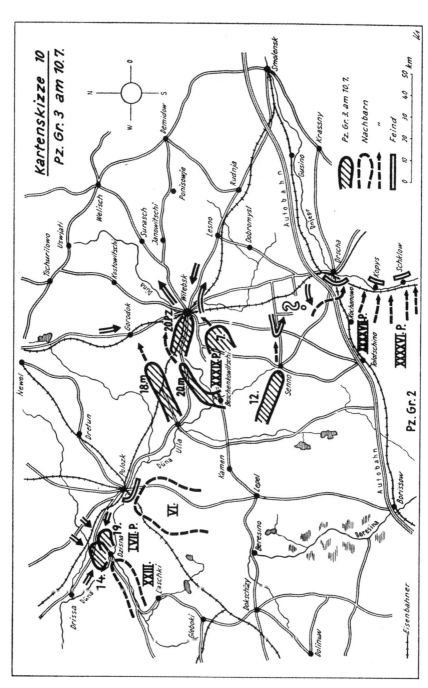

MAP 10: Panzer Group 3 on 10 July

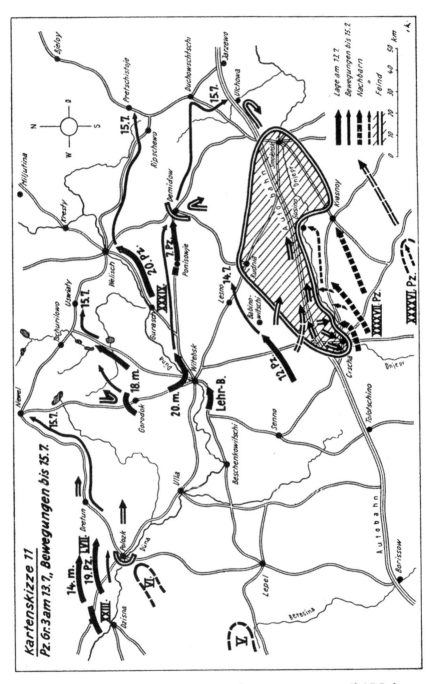

MAP 11: Panzer Group 3 on 13 July, movements until 15 July

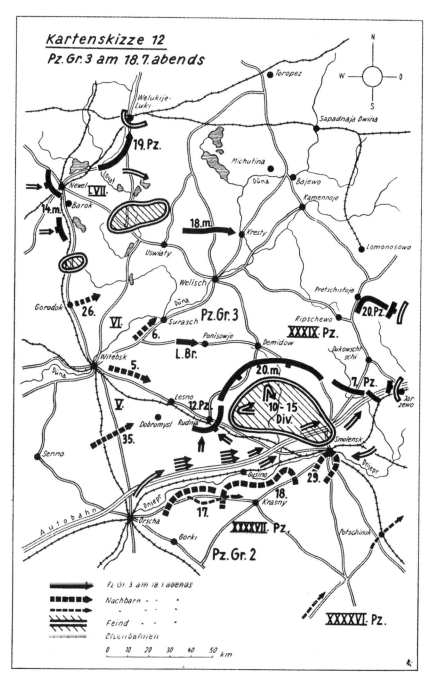

MAP 12: Panzer Group 3 on the evening of 18 July

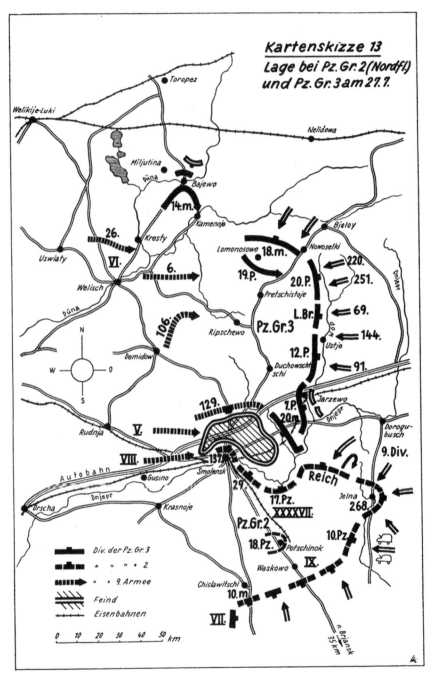

MAP 13: Position of Panzer Group 2 (northern wing)
and Panzer Group 3 on 27 July

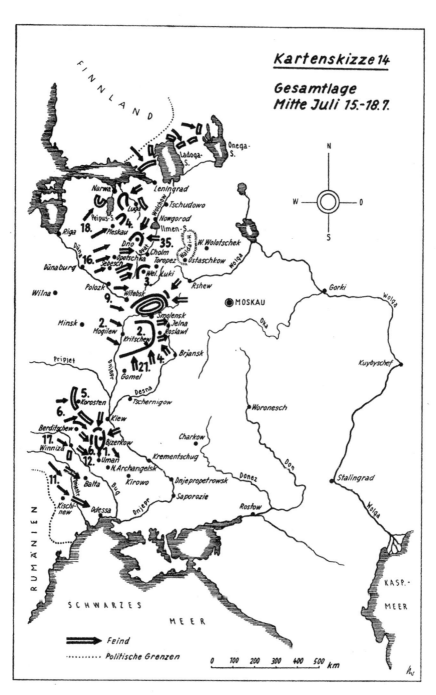

MAP 14: Overall situation, 15–18 July

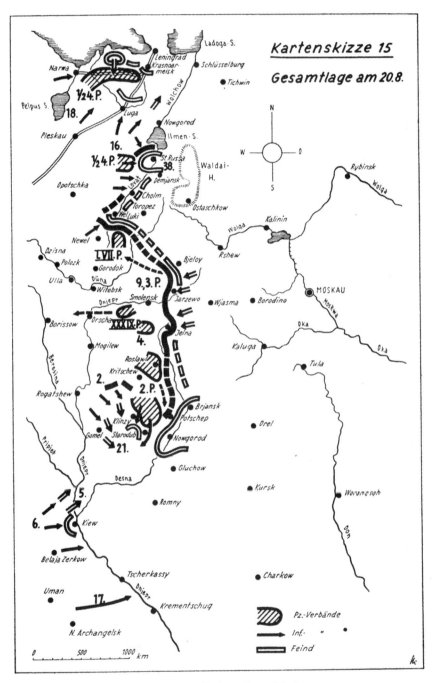

MAP 15: Overall situation, 20 August

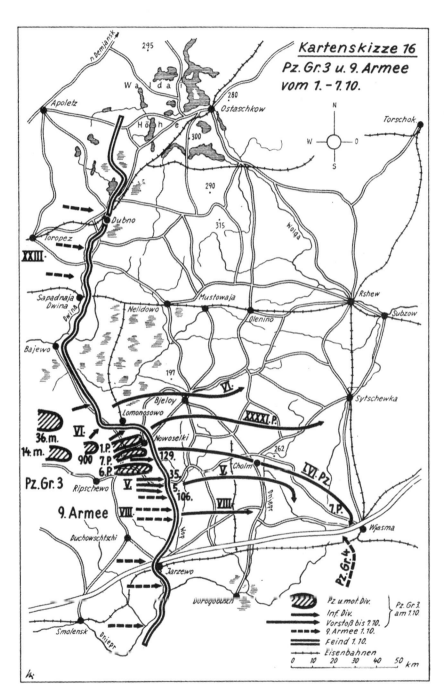

MAP 16: Panzer Group 3 and the Ninth Army, 1–7 October 1941

Select Cities or Geographic Features Seen in the Maps

German	English usage
Brjansk/Briansk	Bryansk
Charkow	Kharkov
Demjansk	Demyansk
r Dnjepr	Dnieper River
e Düna/e Dwina	Western Dvina River
Ilmensee	Lake Ilmen
Jarzewo	Yartsevo
Jelna	Yelnya
Kaspisches Meer	Caspian Sea
Kaukasus	Caucasus
e Krim	Crimea
Ladogasee	Lake Ladoga
Lemberg	Lvov
Mogilew/Mogilhew	Mogilev
Moskau	Moscow
e Moskwa	Moskva River
r Njemen	Neman River
Nowgorod	Novgorod
Ostsee	Baltic Sea
Peipussee	Lake Peipus
Pleskau	Pskov
r Pripjet	Pripyat River
Puszcza Rudnicka	Rudnicka Forest
Rokitnosümpfe	Pripet Marshes
Schwarzes Meer	Black Sea
Slowakei	Slovakia
Tichwin	Tikhvin
Tscherkassy	Cherkassy
Ungarn	Hungary
e Waldaihöhe	Valdai Hills
Warschau	Warsaw
e Weichsel	Vistula River
Wjasma	Vyazma
r Wolga	Volga River

INTRODUCTION

BOUNDARIES BETWEEN TACTICS, OPERATIONS, AND STRATEGY

Anyone who wants to study the history of war not only for pure research but also to draw lessons from it for future wars must deal with the problem of the dramatic extent to which the use of nuclear weapons has changed warfare. Are the lessons from the experiences of previous wars still valid for future wars? Given the technical developments in military affairs, popular opinion readily answers this question with an emphatic 'No'. To refute these naysayers, products of an age uninclined to accept eternal values, it is insufficient to simply assert that doctrines drawn from previous wars remain relevant. Doubters of the value of war experiences contend that the air force, currently bearing the decisive new weapons of destruction (the atomic and hydrogen bombs), has shifted from the role of an auxiliary force to become the 'vital factor in overall strategy', at least in the first phase of war.

These new weapons will not influence all aspects of warfare to the same degree. They will probably more strongly determine strategy and tactics than operations. Since we will deal with 'operations' in this book, it is necessary to define this term.

Clausewitz[1] only distinguished between strategy and tactics: terms like 'base of operations' and 'line of operations' he classified as strategy, and 'marches' as strategy or tactics. His aversion to anything reminiscent of the 'art of manoeuvre' of the eighteenth century led him to neglect operational movements. In non-military circles the term 'strategic' was often applied where the soldier would mostly use 'tactical'. From the nineteenth century onwards, especially in Germany, the increasing complexity of warfare (i.e. the expansion of the theatres of war, the supply of large armies, the ever-increasing predominance of technology, the all-new military arms like the air force, and the disintegration of the former political, parliamentary, economic, and military unity in the conduct of war) led to the elevation of strategy to a higher level than Clausewitz had in mind and to the separation of the term 'operational doctrine' and its classification between tactics and strategy.

Of the now-existing three terms (strategy, operations, and tactics), the most clearly defined is 'tactics'. It is actually the area of the fight and the fighter. Clausewitz described tactics as 'the theory of the use of armed forces in combat'.[2] This corresponds to our present view, although the tactical sphere has expanded spatially and temporally. Today the tactical action begins not on the first day of battle but with the influence of the air force beforehand. And we still see the battle, which rages on broad fronts and drags on for days and weeks, as a tactical whole, while modern means of communication permit personal command from the longest distances.

The line between 'tactics' and 'operations' is rather sharply defined. In contrast the transition from 'strategy' to 'operations' is blurred. Clausewitz's description of strategy, 'the theory of the use of combat for the purpose of war',[3] seems narrow and dogmatic. The main area of strategy is, as Clausewitz points out, the war plan. Taking into account the forces to be deployed and the potential reactions of other countries, the war plan identifies the purpose and goal of the war, and seeks to establish the centre of power, capabilities, and weaknesses of the hostile nation, as well as the strength of will of its government, in order to determine the focal point against which to concentrate one's own efforts. As can be seen, the main part of strategy is subject to political considerations. This cannot be otherwise, because 'policy has produced war'.[4] Erroneous assessments in the war plan, or even the lack of a war plan, will have dire consequences unable to be offset by any military means. Hitler has rightly been blamed for having no clear idea in 1940 as to how to continue and end the war after the quick defeat of France.[5] The opportunity to attack England with the combined strength of the army, navy, and air force immediately after the capitulation of France could not be exploited, because no preparations had been made for a landing operation.

Strategy, and thus politics, not only determines the planning of war but also affects its course. Since war is only decided by the final result, it is for strategy to ensure that the ultimate goal (generally the overthrow of the enemy) is kept in mind, that the collective thrust against the heart of the hostile power is not weakened by considerations for minor operations, that the main battle promising a decisive victory is sought, and that the successful battle is vigorously pursued.

Here we arrive at the border area between 'strategy' and 'operations', and thus also the always controversial subject of disputes over responsibilities between politics and warfare. The soldier who willingly accepts the predominance of politics in strategy will be inclined to say that political considerations cease at the border of 'operations', i.e. the absence of the political element virtually characterises the operational sphere. But it is not so simple. The halt that Bismarck ordered for operations in Bohemia in 1866 encountered stiff resistance from his military-minded King, but seems justified to us today. Another example may help us further: political, ideological, and military factors informed Hitler's decision in the fall of 1940 to temporarily abandon a resolution of the war against England and to attack Russia. This decision was strategic. The directives for the conduct of war against Russia (the 'Barbarossa Order') included the goal of the war, the orders for the three armed services, as well as political and economic considerations. These 'directives' were strategic in nature, even though they were based on the proposals of the High Command of the Army (OKH). However, the 'Deployment Directive for Barbarossa', which the OKH issued on 31 January 1941 on the basis of the Barbarossa Order, was operational in nature.

Strategy is therefore the domain of the highest leadership in war. It is not the subject of our study, but cannot be eliminated from the account of the operations of the army in the summer of 1941.

We will now try to clarify the concept of 'operations'. It usually includes the events of a single theatre of war pursuant to a campaign plan or operational design. Initially there are the 'deployment orders',[6] which essentially contain the strength and organisation of the forces allocated for the campaign, the operational objective to be achieved by the campaign, the probable strength and organisation of the opposing army, and the orders for the subordinate formations and reserves. According to the teaching of Moltke the elder, an operational plan does not usually last beyond the first encounter with the enemy.

'Operations' develop from the 'deployment', i.e. the advance of the prepared forces into battle. Classic examples are the campaigns of Moltke in 1866 and 1870–71, and the long-range movements in the American Civil War. In particular, the 1870–71 campaigns in France guided generations of German military leaders. Through rapid and audacious operations, culminating in decisive battles, the war was ended before the soldiers could fall victim to political fear of the intervention of foreign powers. Based on this experience of war, the notion of bold, decisive operations firmly took root in the German army. However, in his final years the victorious Moltke wrestled with doubts over whether future wars, mobilising whole nations with mass armies against each other, could still be terminated by the same means as the wars of 1866 and 1870–71. He wondered if political means would become necessary to make prospective opponents desire peace.[7] The First World War confirmed Moltke's concerns: trench warfare on the Western Front left little room for operations. In interwar Germany, the effort to regain operational freedom in warfare led to the formation of armoured units with operational, not tactical, tasks. Such operations are the subject of the present analysis.[8]

NUCLEAR WAR

Having outlined the term 'operations' in more detail, we can talk about the changes we can expect in a future war, particularly in regard to the operations of armoured units.

This is not a question of giving a thorough account of atomic theory and nuclear war. Rather, our intention is to examine to what degree the operational use of armoured formations has changed due to the effect of nuclear missiles and bombs on field objectives. For this we must cross over into the neighbouring areas of strategy and tactics in order to understand the influence of nuclear weapons on warfare.

IMPACT ON POLITICS AND STRATEGY

The atomic bomb originally had a strategic purpose. It was supposed to make the Japanese Empire, already defeated at sea and in the air, quickly sue for peace. The news about the vast destructive power of a single bomb made a tremendous impression on the global population. They thought there would be a complete change in warfare. It seemed possible to force large empires into submission with only a few explosions and without the use of troops, but this illusion faded with the realisation that not only *one* world power possessed nuclear bombs. The Korean War, which unfolded as a conventional war, raised doubts as to whether the use of the atomic bomb as in 1945 would be the rule. A well-known British military writer, who cannot be accused of underestimating the influence of technology on warfare, wrote in 1953: 'If wars continue to be waged, nuclear weapons will indeed modify methods but will not change fundamental tactics, or at least no more than the invention of gunpowder did.'[9]

Nevertheless, the effects of the mere existence of the atomic bomb on international relations cannot be overestimated. These effects shall only be listed here insofar as they are of military-political importance.[10] Only a state with the capacity to produce nuclear weapons can claim the rank of a great power. No longer is any state unassailable, nor is neutrality defensible. This will force all states to become great powers. The function of the atomic bomb as a deterrent has become uncertain because one knows neither the power of the atomic bomb of the prospective opponent nor the measure of the moral sense of responsibility with which he intends to use it. The threat of nuclear war, applied with an unscrupulous policy, turns the atom bomb from a deterrent into a tool for blackmail. This introduces an unprecedented element of uncertainty into the politics of nations. The temptation is greater than ever for a major power to launch a pre-emptive war in order to extricate itself from this debilitating lack of freedom of political will. Meanwhile, spreading among the peoples of the world is the fear of an imminent conflict that can engulf everyone in destruction.

Even within the strategic field, nuclear weapons cause fundamental changes in military planning and deployment. The emphasis of strategic considerations is obviously transferred to conducting, and defending against, strategic air warfare. Time and space have together become crucial. The limitless destructive power of atomic bombs in strategic air warfare brings with it, for those who use them first, an otherwise unobtainable advantage. The surprise of a strategic raid plays a far greater role than before, necessitating a substantial increase in the readiness of the armed forces for war. Mobilisation in the former sense will rarely occur. Even deployment methods will be affected. Troops concentrated along railways, along country roads, and in barracks would be victims of a nuclear war. All considerations based on deployment become unreliable in view of the impossibility of foreseeing the results of the preceding strategic raid by nuclear weapons.

Therefore, the effects of nuclear war on strategy are extensive: they impact not only on preparations for war and the outbreak of war, but also on the entire course of the war, especially its goal. Our brief overview must be enough to recognise the profound transformation of strategy. But, of course, the need for the expertise of the military commander in the art of war has not diminished. Aside from his innate wealth of ideas, intuitive grasp of reality, and highly imaginative agility of mind, nuclear war requires from the commander the ability to penetrate the smoke of uncertainty, to see everything clearly, to act decisively, and to remain steadfast under all circumstances. The responsibility placed upon his shoulders is greater than ever.

THE EFFECTS OF NUCLEAR WEAPONS ON THE BATTLEFIELD

The strategic use of the atomic bomb, which would give war such an inhuman character, is not, as previously thought, the only way in which to exploit nuclear power for the purposes of warfare. Given the qualitative balance of nuclear armament, it may even be doubtful whether any power will be the first off the mark to risk launching an all-out nuclear war against population and industrial centres. Less doubtful, however, is the use of tactical nuclear weapons against military targets, since the firepower in ground warfare is now considerably enhanced by the appearance of atomic cannons. While the imagination remains unbounded in assessing the potential of strategic nuclear war, there is now information available on the scientific precision of the atomic cannon against targets in the field, based on the results of tests by American forces.[11] In order to gain an idea of the effect of nuclear projectiles, some technical data are essential. We stick to essentials based on the 28-centimetre atomic cannon with a range of 30 kilometres. It is capable of firing six 20-kiloton projectiles per hour, where a kiloton (kt) is the detonation force of 1000 tons of TNT. Six 20-kt projectiles per hour correspond to the effect of 33,000 medium-calibre field guns in the same amount of time. This is obviously a very crude comparison, since normal artillery fire is more adaptable to terrain and objectives. Nevertheless, there are three factors which make a nuclear projectile effective: the shock wave, the heat, and the radiation. Upon the detonation of the atomic bombs in 1945, the shock wave accounted for 55% of the losses, mostly indirectly through collapsing buildings and hurled-away objects. On the battlefield, the deadly effect of the shock wave will be relatively low, especially with the protection of foxholes and escarpments. It is fatal only in the immediate vicinity of ground zero (point on the surface of the earth directly beneath the point of detonation). Tanks already at some distance (more than 1000 metres) will not be destroyed.

Most losses on the battlefield will be caused by burns, predominantly on the unprotected parts of the body. A bare-chested soldier in the open is at risk even at a distance of 2200 metres. A soldier at a distance of approximately 1000 metres will have time to find a foxhole for protection against the heat wave, while heavy tanks will be almost invulnerable.

The hazard generated by radiation seems to be greatly exaggerated. The radiation from the blast lasts only momentarily. Inside 500 metres it is absolutely deadly. Tanks could safely outrun the immediate vicinity of ground zero within a few minutes after the detonation.

As a general rule it can be said that unprotected troops within a radius of 1600 metres from ground zero will suffer heavy casualties from one of the above-mentioned three factors, whereas a distance of 3000 metres involves no danger for sheltered infantry.

These figures show the tremendous intensification of firepower in the tactical use of nuclear projectiles of standard size. Further intensification by increasing the size is unlikely because one's own troops, deprived of control of the radiation, would be endangered. Moreover, you do not use a howitzer to crack a nut.

The most important conclusion seems to be that tactical defence is stronger than the attack, since the defender, with dugouts and loose formations, can better evade the effects of a nuclear strike than the attacker, who cannot do without a certain concentration of forces at the decisive point. However, this conclusion is debatable. It depends on whether one, despite the threat from nuclear weapons, grants the attacker the opportunity of introducing superior forces where he seeks a decision. We thus touch on the area of operations and will now investigate the alleged influence of nuclear weapons on the operations of armoured units.

OPERATIONS OF ARMOURED UNITS UNDER
THE INFLUENCE OF NUCLEAR WEAPONS

By embarking on an investigation of the operational sphere we depart from experimental facts and become dependent on our own reflections. Insofar as it concerns aircraft as carriers of the atomic bomb, we can draw on the experiences from the last war, as air superiority over enemy territory will generally be a precondition for dropping atomic bombs. For the operations described in this book, air superiority was clearly on the German side in the early days. Even if the enemy had possessed atomic bombs, at that stage the operations would have hardly taken a different course.

Far more than in the past, ground operations and armoured units will depend upon the success of maintaining air superiority, at least in certain areas for short times. But this knowledge is not fundamentally new. The landing operations of the Allies in the summer of 1944 could only succeed because their air force dominated the air space well behind German lines. New methods had to be found for bringing German armoured units to the battlefield at the landing sites.

So aerial bombing is not a new problem with which operations are confronted. This problem did not emerge clearly in the first few years of the Second World War, and the advance of armoured formations took place without taking into account the threat from the air because the enemy was prevented from using its air force effectively. Such immobilisation of an enemy air force will be desirable in future wars.

But if an advancing armoured unit is caught in the effective range of a nuclear bomb, then the damage is naturally much greater than that of a high-explosive bomb, particularly in the vicinity of ground zero. The instantaneous casualties from burning, the shock wave, and the blast radiation, as well as the destruction of material will be more extensive and sustained than with high-explosive bombs. The loss of armoured troops will be lower than that of the infantry because tanks, and even unarmoured vehicles, provide some protection against burning and radiation. The long, narrow line of an advancing column means that a significant portion of the violent impact of an atomic bomb is ineffective in the intermediate area. Above all, after the effect of the shock wave has been overcome and the march route has been cleared, an armoured unit, impervious to contamination, will be able to continue its advance. Only a large number of atomic bombs distributed along the length of an entire column would be effective.

In summary one can probably say that nuclear warfare will not bring tank operations to a standstill if steps are taken to reduce casualties to a tolerable level, i.e. by changing the organisation of formations. Disciplined and widely dispersed formations will avoid a congestion of vulnerable targets within a small area, meaning there will no longer be massed deployments to set up a focal point of main effort. The movement of armour by night on bad roads in inclement weather must be enabled by appropriate vehicle equipment and training. Nevertheless, the essential characteristics of armoured operations (mobility, speed, surprise, and decisive leadership) gain significance in nuclear warfare.

Our account would be incomplete if we did not at least mention the problem of the guided missile (instead of the aircraft) as the main carrier of an atomic projectile, and its influence on warfare. Guided missiles are still in technical development: clearly, despite their supersonic speed, they have not kept pace with explosive materials. Not only are missiles a new element in warfare; their significance basically lies in the shortening of the time factor, i.e. the increased possibility of strategic and tactical surprise.[12]

For our examination of military history, it must suffice to say that the value of past experiences for future wars will depend on the development of guided missiles.

THE STUDY OF MILITARY HISTORY

We thus believe that, while the planning and execution of operations must take into consideration the use of nuclear weapons, the study of earlier operations has not been rendered useless by nuclear warfare. We have now yet to present the methods by which we will study our chosen operations.

Our analysis is based on unused documents, and draws on the memoirs of participants who are still alive, providing some useful service to the investigation of the truth and thus to original war historiography. But that is, as already said, not our real concern.

Since Scharnhorst and Clausewitz, the view is presented in the German army that the science of war is an empirical science; that it is not a system of theorems strung together, but rather applied war history. As a student of Scharnhorst in the Prussian Military Academy, the twenty-four-year-old Clausewitz passionately opposed the idea that a general 'must be a learned historian'. He argued that it was completely irrelevant whether or not one knew individual historical facts.[13] He saw historical studies as an intellectual pursuit, and always remained sceptical when someone wanted to prove a general truth with an illustration from a historical event. As grounds for his scepticism he cited the bold opening of Napoleon's campaign against the Austrians in northern Italy in 1796, which may have appeared as 'glorious decisiveness, but also as true recklessness'.[14] We will have to be all the more on our guard against any overestimation in our account, as we could support such a general truth with insufficient documentary evidence.

The thoughtful Scharnhorst, whose mindset stemmed from the rationalism of the eighteenth century, sought in military history a more real benefit than did his pupil, who created his own ideas. Scharnhorst remodelled in a revolutionary way the existing war historiography, which had previously tended to portray heroes in their most thrilling moments, and we must beware of reverting to this vanquished method. He demanded that 'past events are on the whole understood not as the actions of particular individuals, but as a result of their circumstances'.[15] By immersing ourselves in the campaign plans, the commands, and the considerations of leading personalities, insofar as they are available in records, the reasons for the success or failure of an operation can be discovered. It can lead to disastrous errors if the military leader believes that he can rely on his own experience without the use of military history. The comparison of many examples from war with one another, the detection of errors, the similarity of circumstances, and the multitude of experiences that no single individual could have; only these give him natural competence in the assessment of military situations. Scharnhorst's teaching on pragmatism at the Military Academy asserted that he who disputes the skills needed for a bold decision, who 'derives their own doctrine only from their own observations', who 'is irresolute and fearful of doing something . . . not previously done in their own career . . . ; may never venture a bold idea, because he is unaware of any similar historical case which would give him the necessary self-confidence'.[16]

The 'art of the study and application of useful examples' shaped the teaching of military history in the German general staff. Classes involved the teacher selecting and accurately describing a particular operational position from the course of an exemplary campaign, and the student was required to independently formulate a quick decision based on this position. This method strengthened the student's power of judgement. There is no denying the fact that such instruction with isolated examples entailed the risk of providing only recipes and of neglecting the big picture in war. Scharnhorst's request that 'the physical and moral state of peoples had to be included' in the study of military history was rarely fulfilled. Although these factors fall mainly within the field of strategy, an awareness of them will not prevent us from understanding operations.

The aim of our exposition is to describe, in the sense of Clausewitz, a particular operation in order to give an idea of the principles of its leadership, and to convey, in the sense of Scharnhorst, knowledge about the command of armoured formations which could be applicable under other circumstances. However, we also believe that Jakob Burckhardt's reminder holds true for the study of military history: 'the study of history makes us wiser forever'. Clearly, we can only provide a comprehensive and accurate account by a thorough scrutiny of the sources.

·····························

TWO

BACKGROUND

ORIGINS OF THE OPERATIONAL PLAN

The pros and cons of an attack against Russia are thoroughly described elsewhere;[17] the close interrelationship between politics and warfare which would need to be discussed is beyond the scope of this book. However, we must try to understand how Hitler envisioned the defeat of Russia and how the organisation appointed to implement his intentions, the High Command of the Army (OKH), would put his ideas into action. Specifically, the OKH had to decide upon which war plan and campaign plan the war would be based. Almost always, as far as we can see, the war plan was not stipulated in writing. It was the subject of proposals from the top military leaders and of their meetings with Hitler.

The commander in chief of the army, Field-Marshal Walther von Brauchitsch, had learnt in a meeting with Hitler on 21 July 1940 that the latter was toying with the idea of attacking Russia. Brauchitsch had been instructed 'to tackle the Russian problem and to make theoretical preparations'.[18] Quite unexpectedly, the German general staff was confronted with a task of the kind that it had not dealt with for 25 years. Without even knowing the objective of such a war, Brauchitsch began preparations. By as early as 26 July 1940 the head of Foreign Armies East (ГПО), Lieutenant-Colonel Eberhard Kinzel, reported to the chief of staff of the army, Colonel-General Franz Halder, the basic principles for such an operation. Kinzel concluded that 'the best operational option is to head along the Baltic Sea, veer towards Moscow, and then, from the north, compel Russian forces in the Ukraine and by the Black Sea into battle with a reversed front'.[19] The next day the chief of the operations branch of the general staff, Colonel Hans von Greiffenberg, suggested a strong southern army group. In contrast to both, Halder preferred a strong northern group which would advance directly towards and take Moscow before confronting enemy forces in the south.[20] On 29 July Halder summoned Major-General Erich Marcks, the chief of staff of the Eighteenth Army (the formation with the most troops then stationed in the east), to Berlin and assigned him the task of designing an operational plan against Russia. Meanwhile Hitler, who had originally intended to attack Russia in the autumn, had been notified by Brauchitsch that the deployment of troops on the eastern border would take four to six weeks, and that the aim of the operation would be 'to defeat the Russian army or at least to occupy enough Russian territory to prevent enemy bombers from reaching Berlin and the Silesian industrial area'.[21]

On 31 July Hitler spoke about his intentions in more detail, as recorded by Halder:

> He still would have preferred to attack Russia this year. But this would be impossible, as the campaign would continue into the winter. A standstill would be cause for concern. The operation only makes sense if we crush the Russian state in one go. The objective is the destruction of the vitality of Russia. Gaining territory alone is insufficient. The operations must be divided into two parts: (1) Thrust along the Dnieper towards Kiev. (2) Attack through the Baltic states towards Moscow. Finally, conduct a pincer operation from north and south.

Hitler thought 120 German divisions sufficient for the campaign, leaving 60 divisions for occupied Norway, France, Belgium, and Holland.[22]

On 1 August 1940 the highly regarded Marcks presented to Halder the result of his study, which was written up on 5 August 1940 as 'Operation East'.[23] It served as the preliminary basis for the campaign plan against Russia, though would be altered by further considerations, changes in the political situation, and Hitler's interventions. Marcks's central idea remained: the army would launch the main attack from northern Poland and East Prussia against Moscow in order to destroy the opposing Russian northern group. 18 mobile units and 50 infantry divisions were earmarked for this attack, including an attached army of three armoured divisions and twelve infantry divisions to cover the northern flank between Pskov and Leningrad. An attack against Russian forces in the Ukraine was already 'unavoidable' due to the need to protect the Romanian oilfields. Because of the then still unclear political situation in Romania as well as the few deployment opportunities in southern Poland, only limited forces could be assembled south of the Pripet Marshes. 11 mobile and 24 infantry divisions were allocated in 'Operation East'. Their main objective was Kiev. A strong army reserve of 8 mobile and 36 infantry divisions would primarily support the German northern group.

Once in possession of Moscow and northern Russia, the German northern group would turn southwards and, in a second combat operation alongside the southern group, conquer the Ukraine and ultimately reach the desired Rostov-Gorky-Arkhangelsk line.

In response to Marcks's plan, Halder emphasised that the use of Romanian territory was still uncertain (although an army initially stationed in Germany was transferred to Romania after the start of the campaign), and that the Moscow group would have to treat the seizure of the Baltic states as only a secondary operation.[24] Marcks was instructed to deal with the organisational implications of the proposed plan.

A few other senior general staff officers had outlined their ideas on conducting a war against Russia. We do not know what influence they or the study of the Operations Staff of the Armed Forces (WFSt) in September 1940 exerted on the final plan.

On 3 September 1940 the new Head Quartermaster I, Major-General Friedrich Paulus, was entrusted with conducting war games for the OKH. He recorded his observations in a memorandum on 29 October 1940.[25]

Besides these theoretical studies, troop movements from the west to the eastern frontier, completed on 26 October 1940, ensured security in the face of Russian troop concentrations and facilitated the future deployment for the eastern campaign. On 5 December 1940 Halder presented the outcome of the previous studies on the campaign plan to Hitler. This presentation was followed on 18 December 1940 by Führer Directive No. 21 (Operation Barbarossa) with the main orders for the war against Russia.

THE MILITARY AND POLITICAL SITUATION

Meanwhile, a series of military and political events had occurred. Russia expanded northwards by incorporating the Baltic states into its sphere of influence after having already annexed Bessarabia and Northern Bukovina in June 1940. A German-Italian arbitration in Vienna on 30 August forced Romania to cede considerable territory to Hungary. At the same time, Germany assumed responsibility for the guarantee of the Romanian border and dispatched to Romania, with the consent of its government, a military mission, a motorised infantry division reinforced with tanks, and 'instruction units' of the air force, whose task it would be 'to protect the Romanian oil fields from access or destruction by a third power' and to prepare for the deployment of German and Romanian troops from Romania against Russia.[26] In August 1940 the German armaments programme, due to the possibility of a Russian war, switched from reducing production to increasing the number of divisions by 180, including 20 armoured divisions and 17 motorised infantry divisions. The Battle of Britain, which began at the end of August, led not to an invasion of England but to severe material losses for the German air force. Consequently, at the end of September the goal of landing on the island had to be postponed. In contrast, the conquest of the Atlantic coast by German troops significantly reduced English shipping space. Negotiations with Spain regarding an occupation of Gibraltar progressed no further beyond the end of October. On 27 September 1940 Germany, Italy, and Japan concluded a tripartite pact with far-reaching political goals. In September Italy started an offensive in North Africa which ended in early December with a decisive defeat by British troops, making German support necessary. In the Balkans, Italy attacked Greece from Albania with inadequate forces. The Greek counterattack threw the Italians back into Albania, while English auxiliary troops landed in Greece and Crete, requiring Germany to consider the deployment of eight divisions to the Balkans. On 12 November in Berlin, German negotiations with Vyacheslav Molotov, the Russian foreign minister, proceeded unsatisfactorily.

Compared with the summer, when the world seemed to hold its breath after the rapid defeat of France, the military-political situation of Germany, unbeknown to its people, had deteriorated considerably because of the failure of the German air offensive against England, the Italian setbacks in Libya and the Balkans, the idleness of the German land forces, and the strained Russo-German relations. Confidence in the absolute superiority of the German army continued unabated, and the food situation thanks to the regular supplies from Russia, was satisfactory. Very few people, even in the army, foresaw the imminence of war against Russia.

Under these conditions the key operational decisions had to be made in the first half of December 1940 in case of a war on two fronts.

BARBAROSSA

Halder's aforementioned presentation to Hitler on 5 December 1940 dealt almost exclusively with the question of how to convincingly smash the units of the Red Army stationed in western Russia. Halder referred to the well-known fact that this part of Russia was divided into two by the Pripet Marshes, and suggested positioning the greater part (two army groups) of the German eastern army to the north of these marshes, while in the south an army group of German and Romanian formations would penetrate into the Ukraine. Halder added:

> The road network south of the Pripet Marshes is bad. The best roads and railways are in the Warsaw-Moscow region. The northern half of the theatre of operations therefore offers more favourable conditions for large-scale movement than the southern half. Here we will probably also confront the bulk of the Russian army. The enemy must be forced into battle to the west of the Dnieper-Dvina line to prevent him from protecting his armaments industries in the Ukraine, Moscow, and Leningrad. Armoured spearheads should tear the front wide open and crush further resistance. The main thrust in this connection should be conducted by the middle of the three army groups from Warsaw in the direction of Moscow. The ultimate objective of the entire operation is to reach the Volga and Arkhangelsk.[27]

Other operational possibilities were apparently not discussed.

Hitler expressed his agreement. He had apparently abandoned his thoughts of 31 July 1940, a large-scale envelopment from the northern and southern flanks. Nevertheless, he raised a new problem which would greatly influence the operations in the summer of 1941. 'In the north the encirclement of the enemy forces stationed in the Baltics is desirable. For this the centre should be of sufficient strength so that it can wheel northwards; only later can it be decided whether to advance on Moscow or into the region east of the city.' Hitler emphasised that powerful enemy forces should be destroyed in the initial stage so that the Russians could not form a united front. The invasion was to extend as far east as possible so that the territory of the Reich would be protected from attacks by the Red Air Force, and so that it would be possible for the German air force to obliterate Russian industrial areas. In this way the annihilation of the Russian armed forces had to be achieved and their regeneration prevented.[28]

On 17 December 1940 the chief of the WFSt, General of the Artillery Alfred Jodl, presented to Hitler the draft for Operation Barbarossa. It did not meet with Hitler's approval since it was based on the operational plan of the OKH, to conduct the main attack through Smolensk towards Moscow, and not on his expressed intention from 5 December, to commence with an encirclement of the enemy in the Baltics.[29] Specifically, he stated that:

> The Russian front is to be penetrated with the main effort on both sides of the Pripet Marshes, gaining territory to the east with heavy motorised forces in order to pivot to the north and south. A northwards pivot is particularly necessary so as to provide cover against the enemy counterattacks expected from the east. The Baltic Sea region must also be taken rapidly so that the Russian fleet cannot disrupt ore imports from Sweden to Germany. If the Russian army disintegrates very quickly, it will be possible for the centre, in addition to swinging northwards, to advance on Moscow.[30]

The operation had to be altered accordingly, and Hitler's remarks were conveyed to Brauchitsch on 21 December.

Meanwhile, Brauchitsch had received Hitler's Directive No. 21 (Operation Barbarossa). This directive has already been published verbatim elsewhere,[31] so only those sections relevant to the operations discussed here are reiterated. The German armed forces had to prepare for the means by which to 'overthrow Soviet Russia in a quick campaign'. The directive continued:

> The bulk of the Russian army stationed in western Russia should be destroyed in bold operations by driving forward with armoured spearheads, while the withdrawal of combat-effective

units into the depths of the Russian empire must be prevented. In quick pursuit a line is then to be reached from which the Russian air force can no longer attack German territory. The ultimate objective of the operation is to defend the Reich against Asiatic Russia from the Volga-Arkhangelsk line. Thus the last industrial area in Russia, in the Urals, can if necessary be eliminated by the German air force. [Army Group Centre was assigned the task of] advancing with powerful armoured and motorised formations from the area around and north of Warsaw, and shattering the enemy forces in Belarus. This will enable heavy mobile troops to turn northwards and, in conjunction with the northern army group operating out of East Prussia in the general direction of Leningrad, to destroy enemy forces in the Baltics. Only after fulfilling this most essential task, including the occupation of Leningrad and Kronstadt, will offensive operations proceed with the capture of the important centre of transportation and armaments production in Moscow.

Only a surprisingly rapid collapse of Russian resistance could justify the simultaneous pursuit of both objectives. . . . The greater part of the Finnish army is assigned the task, in coordination with the advance of the German northern wing, to pin down the strongest possible Russian forces by an attack to the west or on both sides of Lake Ladoga.

The army group operating south of the Pripet Marshes was supposed to attack in the direction of Kiev with a strong northern wing,

advancing quickly with powerful armoured formations and outflanking Russian forces west of the Dnieper . . .

Once the battles to the north and south of the Pripet Marshes are completed, the following will be pursued: in the south the early occupation of the Donets Basin with its important war industry, and in the north the rapid advance on Moscow.

The seizure of this city would represent a politically and economically decisive victory, aside from which Russia would lose its most important railway junction.

CONSIDERATIONS

The WFSt-developed draft for Operation Barbarossa of 18 December 1940 remained significant for the operations of the army in 1941, even though it was circulated six months before the invasion began. The expansion of the Balkan campaign in Serbia in April 1941 entailed a reduction of forces allocated to Army Group South. Meanwhile, Russian forces in Galicia were reinforced. But since the operational orders for Army Group South remained the same, its task became even more difficult. The Balkan campaign required the postponement of Barbarossa from mid-May to 22 June 1941, but its operational tasks and goals did not change.

If we examine the directive for Barbarossa to determine whether it gave the OKH sufficient documentation for the arrangements to be taken, we encounter the distinction used by von Moltke between 'war objective' and 'operational objective'. 'The former deals not with the army but rather the participating countries, the capital of the enemy, and the political power of the state . . . , operational objective, however, concerns the enemy army, which protects the war objective.'[32] Since the campaigns of Frederick the Great it had become an axiom of warfare to make the objective not a geographical point but the enemy army itself, the destruction of which in a decisive battle all operations must be directed towards. On 31 July 1940 Hitler had not left the slightest doubt that the primary goal, 'the operational objective', must be the 'vitality' of the enemy; 'territorial gain is insufficient'. The operational orders took this into account. Economic goals were only to be pursued afterwards. It is noteworthy that the directive for Barbarossa dealt predominantly with operational matters, which were the concern of the commanders, including Brauchitsch, in the Russian theatre of war. However, the orders revealed little on the strategic sphere, especially regarding the 'war objective', though this may have been arranged with Brauchitsch.

Directive No. 21 ordered as the war aim the 'conquest of Soviet Russia'. Later, in August 1941, Hitler declared that the war aim was 'to finally eliminate Russia as a powerful continental ally of England'.[33] These statements were very different and ambiguous in their meanings. Did Hitler know how he wanted to end the war? Clausewitz, who took part in the War of 1812 on the Russian side, afterwards defended Napoleon against the accusation of having advanced too far into Russia:

> The Russian Empire is not a country that can be completely conquered, i.e. that can be permanently occupied. . . . Such a country can only be subjugated by its own weaknesses and by the effects of internal division. In order to strike these weak points of the political existence of Russia, a considerable shock to the heart of the state is necessary. Only when Napoleon persevered with his powerful thrust on Moscow could he hope to shake the courage of the government and the loyalty and steadfastness of the people. He hoped to restore peace in Moscow, the only reasonable goal for which he could aim in this war. . . . The campaign of 1812 failed because the enemy government was unyielding and retained the support of its people.[34]

Did this observation, which was made when the Russian people were politically unenlightened and mystically devoted to Tsardom, remain true in 1940 regarding Bolshevik tyranny? Would the forces of the fledgling Bolshevik state cope with the tremendous demands of a struggle for existence or inexistence? Was Bolshevism already so deeply rooted in the Russian people that it was ready to make the greatest sacrifices in its defence, or would military defeat also mean the end of Bolshevik tyranny? Would the numerous national minorities of the complex Russian realm use the opportunity to regain their autonomy? And finally, would Stalin, the cool and level-headed statesman, find his rule in jeopardy under the effect of a desperate military situation, or would he be prepared to negotiate? These were questions that the soldier could not answer, as they profoundly encroached upon the political objective of the war. Nevertheless, the operational goals also depended on the answers to these questions, but they remained unanswered in what was a fundamentally strategic directive. Operations even had to be coordinated with wartime economic objectives. The latter could not be dealt with subsequently.

Behind the active Russian army, which it was hoped could be defeated west of Dnieper-Dvina, stood ten million reservists, though they first had to be armed and trained. Quite differently to the time of Moltke, technology, industry, and the economy had become part of the 'political power of the state' and were thus war objectives. The appraisal of these objectives and of their prospects of boosting the fighting capacity of the enemy had to be the focus of strategic considerations. As important as the annihilation of the active army was, what had to ensue was the far more protracted destruction of the enemy's armaments industry. How was the offensive against this war objective supposed to be conducted? The Barbarossa directive counted on the seizure of the Donets Basin and of the industrial areas around Moscow and Leningrad by means of the operations of the army. This was very optimistic. Since the main thrust was supposed to be directed towards Moscow for political reasons, it was questionable whether the available time and strength would be sufficient for the occupation of the Ukraine. The assault against the armaments centres lying further to the east would then fall to the air force. These were utopian ideas. The range of German bombers at that time was 1000 kilometres. Even if the desired Volga-Arkhangelsk line could be reached, impossible in a campaign of only three to four months, the air force would have been unable to bomb the Urals industrial area, the Sverdlovsk district. Moreover, the world did not end at Sverdlovsk. It was known that since 1928 an even mightier industrial centre came into being in Siberia in the Kusnets district which together with the Urals industrial centre comprised 12 percent of the total area of the Soviet Union.

It had to be accepted that despite all victories a 'regeneration' of the Russian army could not be prevented. The only possible conclusion was not to pursue economic goals but to clearly outline the political goal: to weaken the military and political power of Russia so that it would be prepared to negotiate. Moscow would thus need to be both the war objective and operational objective.

Instead of developing a clear strategic foundation for the war against Russia, during the preparatory period Hitler devoted himself to operational planning, an area which was not his concern. The operational plan changed by leaps and bounds. Initially, on 31 July 1940, he had in mind an operation launched from both flanks (towards Kiev and the Baltics). On 5 December 1940 he agreed to the proposed central thrust towards Moscow. On 17 December he expressed his intention to advance far to the east on both sides of the Pripet Marshes and then to converge from north and south. Finally, on 18 December 1940, he had signed the Barbarossa order, which intended the cooperation of both northern army groups in taking the Baltic Sea region and only then driving on Moscow.

Consistent with all of these considerations was this: the war objective was supposed to be achieved in *one* campaign. For Hitler the war only made sense if 'the state was smashed to pieces in one go' (31 July 1940). This urge for a rapid campaign was related to his intentions for further warfare. After the armistice in France took effect on 25 June 1940 the war on land had made no significant progress, and nor would it do so for months. The lightning-fast action of the German army in May and June 1940 stood in stark contrast to the dilatory overall conduct of the war, which gave away a valuable year to the Western powers. Now the upcoming Russian war firmly committed German land forces to the east for 1941. If the war in the east dragged on, England would regain the initiative and the consequences could be disastrous.

Hitler's wish for a repetition of the rapid French campaign in Russia would be frustrated by the very different conditions of warfare in the east, especially the distances to be covered, exacerbated by poor road conditions. Perhaps the available three to four months were sufficient to demolish the active enemy forces and to occupy vast areas of the country, including its capital. But this would not, as we have seen, affect the vitality of Russia. Therefore, the operational objective, if it was to be achieved in *one* campaign, needed to be considered more closely.

So far as we can see, it was Halder who proposed the 'ultimate goal of the campaign, reaching the Volga and Arkhangelsk'. By August 1941 he became aware that this was unattainable.[35]

DEPLOYMENT ORDERS

The OKH spent the following weeks working out the arrangements necessary for the implementation of Directive No. 21, developing by 31 January 1941 the 'Deployment Orders for Barbarossa'.[36] These orders replaced Directive No. 21 as the instructions for the overthrow of Soviet Russia in a quick campaign, and also revised other parts of the directive:

> The first objective of the OKH within the framework of the orders issued is to rip open the front in western Russia, where the bulk of the Russian army is to be expected, with rapid and deep attacks by heavy mobile formations north and south of the Pripet Marshes, and to exploit this breakthrough so as to destroy the separated enemy groups.

Both northern army groups would cooperate in the destruction of the enemy in the Baltic states, as ordered in Directive No. 21, but with less emphasis on the urgency of the capture of Leningrad and Kronstadt before Moscow. Rather, the objective was,

> in conjunction with the Finnish army, to conclusively eliminate the potential for enemy resistance in northern Russia and thereby to ensure freedom of movement for further assignments (possibly in cooperation with German forces in southern Russia). In the event of a surprising and complete collapse of enemy

resistance in the north of Russia, an immediate advance on Moscow without diverting forces may be possible.

The orders for Army Group Centre were formulated in a further passage:

> With strong forces advancing on the wings, Army Group Centre shall crush enemy forces in Belarus, acquire through the combined effort of its mobile forces north and south of Minsk the area around Smolensk, and thus create the prerequisite for the cooperation of heavy mobile troops with Army Group North in the destruction of enemy formations in the Baltic and Leningrad regions.

Following this were the orders for the armies and panzer groups, which will be discussed later.

The deployment orders of 31 January were forwarded to Hitler on 1 February. On 3 February Halder, in the presence of Brauchitsch, spoke to Hitler about its contents. Halder said something like the following:

> Enemy forces near the border are estimated at 125 infantry and cavalry divisions as well as 30 armoured and motorised units. Given the German deployment, 50 infantry and 22 armoured and motorised infantry divisions shall be concentrated north of the Pripet Marshes, while on the southern wing only 30 infantry and 8 armoured and motorised infantry divisions will be formed. The army reserves, 22 infantry and 4 armoured and motorised infantry divisions, will be transported en masse closely behind Army Group Centre. The aim is to split the Russian front into two, and to prevent a retreat to the Dnieper and the Western Dvina. The three panzer groups of Army Groups Centre and North will head north-east towards Smolensk and over the Western Dvina.

The northernmost panzer group is to charge towards Lake Peipus in order to proceed from there further eastwards in coaction with the two other panzer groups.

Army Group South will advance south of the Pripet Marshes towards and over the Dnieper.

Thereupon a number of detailed questions were discussed. Hitler agreed with the objectives, but then said:

The zone of operations is immense. The encirclement of large parts of the Russian army will only succeed if executed without interruption. The immediate surrender of the Baltic states, Leningrad, and the Ukraine is unlikely. However, it is possible that after the initial defeats the Russians, in recognition of the German operational objectives, will conduct a large-scale withdrawal in order to prepare a new defensive line further to the east. In this case the Baltic and Leningrad area must be sorted out regardless of Russian forces further east. From there, instead of a frontal attack, a strike against the rear of the Russians shall then be led. It is essential to destroy a large part of the opponent, not to make him run. We must seize the flanks with the strongest forces while being restrained in the centre so as to then outmanoeuvre the enemy.[37]

In the following months Hitler further occupied himself with operational considerations. These included the protection of the flanks bordering the Pripet Marshes, the coastal defence of Norway, the security of the Petsamo nickel mines, and the Greek campaign, all of which limited the effectiveness of an attack on Russia.

In Berlin on 30 March 1941, three days after the military coup in Belgrade, which extended Germany's Balkan campaign to Serbia, Hitler convened the commanders of the army groups, armies, panzer groups, as well as those of the navy and air force, involved in Operation Barbarossa. By now they had received the deployment orders and had outlined their goals, which were reported separately by each commander in detail. Hitler again stressed the importance of occupying the Baltics: 'We must not allow the Russians to avoid a decisive battle in the border region, particularly in the Baltic states. Whether Panzer Group 4 of Army Group North advances to the Gulf of Riga or moves northwards along Lake Peipus, cutting off the enemy's retreat to the coast, must be decided according to the situation.' Both panzer groups of Army Group Centre (2 and 3) would have to head towards Leningrad after reaching Minsk, which Hitler saw as the ideal solution for the operational problem. He rejected any suggested changes to the deployment orders.

CONSIDERATIONS: LEADERSHIP CRISIS?

Brauchitsch has been accused of not clarifying with Hitler their differences in opinion on how the war against Russia should be conducted.[38] Now, it is certainly true that Brauchitsch did not press strategic and operational issues with Hitler. It is also true that, for Brauchitsch, the primary aim of the war was the destruction not of the Russian economy but of the Russian army. Yet no conflict with Hitler on this matter had previously transpired. Even on 9 January 1941 Hitler had himself identified the destruction of the Russian army as the primary aim, and on 5 December 1940 and 3 February 1941 he had been in agreement with Brauchitsch's proposals. In the course of numerous meetings over the details of the leadership of the operations, for which Brauchitsch was responsible, Hitler had frequently expressed contradictory views. As the calculating Field-Marshal Erich von Manstein precisely put it, Hitler lacked 'military ability based on experience, which his intuition could not replace'.[39]

It is therefore understandable if Brauchitsch did not address all of Hitler's fluctuating operational ideas, particularly as the uselessness of these proposals is now clear.

However, Hitler doggedly asserted that the rapid occupation of the

Baltic states and the annihilation of enemy forces there should be supported by diverting the mobile forces of Army Group Centre northwards. He justified this not only politically and economically but also operationally. The limited area for the assembly and advance of Panzer Group 4 north of the Neman offered little opportunity to encircle the enemy echeloned in depth in the Baltics. Only the complete elimination, rather than expulsion, of enemy forces in the Baltics would provide the northern wing of the army the freedom needed to advance on Moscow. These military considerations may have prompted Brauchitsch to comply, more than he originally wanted, with Hitler's wishes in the deployment orders. Halder's report of 3 February 1941 therefore explicitly stressed the intention of sending three panzer groups in a north-easterly direction over the Western Dvina towards Smolensk so that these strong armoured forces (22 armoured and motorised infantry divisions) could interact. In reality this concentration did not materialise for reasons to be discussed later. On the basis of Halder's report, Hitler could presume that his wishes would be accommodated, and so refrained from further intervention.

The conflict between Hitler and Brauchitsch, the so-called 'leadership crisis', was inflamed in July and August 1941 over a different question, namely Hitler's desire to divert strong forces of Army Group Centre southwards so as to enable Army Group South to conquer the Ukraine. But this was not the issue prior to the war against Russia.

BREAKTHROUGH OR ENVELOPMENT?

At the end of January the OKH estimated that the Russians would have gathered 115 rifle divisions, 25 cavalry divisions, and 31 armoured and motorised units on the border with Germany and Romania. Of these, 84 rifle divisions and 8 armoured units had been identified opposite Romania, Germany, and Finland in mid-March. Thereafter, additional Russian troops steadily moved up to the border. By the beginning of the war with Russia the German leadership expected to encounter approximately 150 rifle and cavalry divisions as well as 40 armoured and motorised units. Since the overall strength of the Russians was assessed in early April at over 250 rifle and cavalry divisions, the initial attack would only harm three-fifths of them.

The forces on both sides faced each other as follows:

On the German side

	INFANTRY DIVISIONS	ARMOURED & MOTORISED DIVISIONS
Army Group South	30	9
Army Group Centre	32 + 1 cavalry division	15
Army Group North	20	6
Army Reserve	22	4
TOTAL	104 + 1 cavalry division	34

On the Russian side

	RIFLE & CAVALRY DIVISIONS	ARMOURED & MOTORISED UNITS
Opposing Army Group South	71	20
Opposing Army Group Centre	44	11
Opposing Army Group North	31	8
Still available	104 (estimated)	
TOTAL	250	39

The German high command favoured a frontal attack with all army groups and hoped, with armoured wedge formations advancing on a broad front, to develop operational freedom of movement, to outflank the enemy, and to prevent his withdrawal to the east. This might have been able to succeed north of the Pripet Marshes, where there was superiority in armoured units, but operational freedom could not be expected for Army Group South due to the more than two-fold superiority of the enemy. This suggests that the idea was to forego an attack by Army Group South and to deploy mobile forces where they could be operationally effective, namely in the north. Such reinforcement of the left wing of the army with mobile units would have made possible the following operation:

After the breakthrough in the direction of Minsk and Dünaburg, the destruction of the enemy's centre, and the consequent gain of operational freedom, the four panzer groups would proceed north-eastwards over the middle Western Dvina into the rear of enemy forces in the Baltics in order to cut off their communications to the east, including Leningrad. The final encirclement of this enemy, with his back against the Baltic Sea, could be entrusted to the infantry corps. The mobile forces would have been strong enough to repel Russian relief attacks over the Valdai Hills and, further south, towards the west. Army Group Centre, now without armour, would be under strict orders to stop at the Dnieper, and to echelon reserves in depth behind the left flank.

Kinzel, in his aforementioned operational proposal to Halder on 26 July 1940, envisaged an attack along the Baltic Sea, heading towards Moscow and then, from the north, forcing the enemy in the Ukraine into battle with an inverted front. At the end of July 1941 such an attack with all of the German armoured divisions, accompanied on the left flank by motorised infantry divisions, could peel southwards from the upper Volga in the Valdai Hills towards Moscow. The continuation of this attack to the south would have very soon cut off the Russian army from the armaments centres in the Urals and to the east. Admittedly, it would have also risked an exposed left flank. It is futile to claim that such an operation could have succeeded or that the war could have been won in this way. However, this example should show the possibilities for bold, large-scale armoured operations if concentrated during deployment against a focal point rather than distributed across the entire front.

ASSESSMENT OF THE RED ARMY IN 1941

The suspected strength of the Red Army has already been discussed. Ever since Hitler had broken off military relations between Germany and Russia, news about the Red Army had been scarce. It was known that from approximately 1928 the Russian army had adopted German training and leadership principles. It was unknown if these principles endured beyond the 1937 liquidation of several high-ranking Russian officers.

The extremely modest Russian soldier, accustomed to making great efforts, was disciplined and trained carefully in the use of weapons. In the utilisation of the land, especially in defence, he was a master. Regarding his likelihood to turn his back on the Bolshevik regime, those in the German army, unlike party officials, laboured under no illusions. It was known that the Russian army, particularly the officer corps, was bound to the regime by considerable state resources (good pay and food, free rent and travel, holidays at health resorts, and well-equipped clubs). Political commissars, sometimes hated and always feared, were perceived as a foreign body, and their influence on the conduct of field operations depended entirely on their personality and that of the commanders. It was doubtful whether the Russian leadership had overcome its ever-inherent tendency for routine and its helplessness in unforeseen circumstances.

The Russian armoured forces were divided into mechanised brigades and a few armoured divisions. Armoured corps did not yet exist. Instead, individual rifle divisions were allocated obsolete tanks. From this organisation it can be concluded that Russia had yet to exploit the operational use of large armoured formations as had Germany during the campaigns in Poland and France.

It could not be said with certainty whether our tank guns were superior to those of the Russians in range and penetration, though we hoped so. Shortly before the eastern campaign began, Hitler himself had received indefinite intelligence of a heavy Russian tank. By early July we encountered it in southeast Vitebsk.

On the whole, the German army commenced military action in the east in the knowledge of its qualitative superiority.

GERMAN PREPAREDNESS FOR WAR IN THE EAST?

Only gradually, from January 1941, were the German commanders made familiar with their new assignments in the east. It turned out that nobody had anticipated the possibility of a war with Russia. Maps and military geographical descriptions of the land were only now produced. They were based in part on carefully detailed, albeit outdated and thus inadequate, descriptions of routes worked on for years before the First World War. In particular, it could only rarely be gathered from the distributed maps which road connections and bridges were useful for motor vehicles and tanks. It was necessary to assign multiple routes without knowing if they would be passable, and to let the troops handle them.

The allotted motor vehicles seemed completely inadequate for warfare in the east. It has already been mentioned that the number of armoured and motorised infantry divisions was doubled after the French campaign. Panzer Group 3, whose operations are covered here, possessed four panzer divisions for every panzer corps. Of these, the 7th Panzer Division had already proven its great worth in the western campaign, the 12th Panzer Division was converted from a motorised infantry division, and the 19th and 20th Panzer Divisions were transformed from infantry divisions. All panzer divisions had, instead of the previous single tank brigade, only one tank regiment of three tank battalions. However, they were now equipped with the Panzer III and IV. So the tank regiment of, for example, the 19th Panzer Division had at its disposal 42 of the Panzer IV, 102 of the Panzer III, 9 of the upgraded Panzer III, and 20 of the Panzer II. The armoured personnel carriers of the new panzer divisions, especially those of the 20th Panzer Division, were of French civilian origin and unsuitable for the routes in the east. Specifically, there was a lack of cross-country motor vehicles. Company commanders had to lead their troops from small sedans. It appeared no better for the motorised infantry divisions. All three motorised infantry divisions (the 14th, 18th, and 20th) had been reorganised from infantry divisions in the winter of 1940-41. They received their vehicles only during the last months preceding the outbreak of war in the east (for the 18th Division it was only a few days).

This provision of vehicles unsuited to the conditions of the eastern terrain must be taken into account in the assessment of the operations.

For further details regarding the order of battle see appendix 9.

THE LAND (MAPS 3, 4, 5, 7, AND 11)

Panzer Group 3 was deployed in East Prussia, approximately in the area Lyck-Marggrabowa-Rastenburg-Sensburg. From there the divisions would head, immediately before the attack, along two roads to the assembly position, the Suwalki region, which Lithuania had ceded to Germany in 1939. The countryside was filled with woods and lakes, and had a well-developed network of roads leading to the Neman. In the attack sector of Panzer Group 3 there were four fixed bridges which crossed this river: two at Olita, and one each at Merkine and Prienai. Beyond the Neman was vast, partly swampy, but mainly low, sandy woodland through which only one road led, via Varena, to the communication road Lida-Vilnius. To the east of this road, between the 'Western' Berezina and its tributaries and the Viliya, a well-cultivated ridge of land stretches from a roughly 300-metre height eastwards through Oshmyany to Smorgon. At its narrowest point lay the railway junction at Molodechno, famous for Napoleon's bulletin of 5 December 1812, in which he announced to the world his well-being and the demise of the Grand Army. The main road from Vilnius ran through Smorgon and Molodechno to Minsk, beyond which the highway led to Smolensk and Moscow.

To the north and south of Molodechno spread marshlands, impassable in summer and offering only a few sandy passages. Only the territory to the north of Lake Naroch is negotiable. Here, a narrow mountain ridge extends past Glubokoye to Polotsk on the Western Dvina.

East of Molodechno the terrain rises considerably, reaching 360 metres to the north of Minsk. Here, east of the former Belarusian-Polish border and facing northwest, the Russians had begun construction on an array of modern and unassailable, yet incomplete, concrete fortifications. The land descends further north towards Dokshitsy and reaches eastwards of Lepel to Vitebsk. From Dokshitsy the 'historic' Berezina flows, via the small village of Beresino, southwards through marshy woodlands to Borisov and Bobruisk, eventually reaching the Dnieper. Not far north of the point where the highway crosses the Berezina were the remnants of the bridge burned down, after the westward retreat of the shattered Grand Army, on 29 November 1812.

East of the Berezina the land ascends slightly. The landscape between the Dnieper and the Western Dvina is interspersed with several small lakes and is deficient in serviceable roads. The Lepel-Vitebsk 'road' and its fork leading to Ula become extremely muddy in the rain.

East of Orsha-Vitebsk-Nevel the land increasingly assumes the character of Inner Russia proper: a vast, slightly undulating plain, a few sprawling villages with wretched and verminous wooden huts, and wide, unmade dirt roads. To the north and south of Demidov the country is open. Potatoes, buckwheat, and occasionally flax grow in miserable fields cultivated mostly by women. Then dense woodland covers the terrain to the Yartsevo-Dukhovshchina-Prechistoye 'road'.

The Vitebsk-Nevel road is, strikingly, largely paved, while the Smolensk-Vitebsk and Vitebsk-Velizh roads are tolerable. Approaching the headwaters of the Western Dvina in the direction of Velikiye Luki and Toropets, the sand becomes deeper and the sparse roads more abysmal. Here, within the borderland of Russia proper, the land is deliberately neglected in order to deter intruders. For a long time it would be the zone of operations for Panzer Group 3.

SUSPECTED ORGANISATION OF ENEMY FORCES
BEFORE PANZER GROUP 3 AND ADJACENT UNITS

German reconnaissance had located three Russian divisions opposite the Suwalki region between the frontier and the Neman. It was believed that most of their troops were billeted and echeloned in depth behind field fortifications defending the border. Southwest of Kalvarija enormous concrete works were under construction. They were obviously vulnerable. It was suspected that an armoured division lay to the east of Olita. There was no sign that the Nemen would be adequately defended. The entire area around the Lida-Vilnius road appeared to be devoid of troops. Expected here was the border between the central and northern Russian fronts (commanded by Marshals Semyon Timoshenko and Kliment Voroshilov respectively). The forces in Kovno and Vilnius probably belonged to the northern front.

South of Panzer Group 3 Russian territory protruded far westwards. There were strong forces, even motorised, in this 'Bialystok salient', more than seemed necessary for defensive purposes. These forces, dispersed all the way to Minsk, were the first operational objective of Army Group Centre, and were to be enveloped from the north and south.

Also, to the north of Panzer Group 3 the Russians guarded the border with a loose formation, although most of the divisions covering the Baltics stood far to the east of the Western Dvina. It was impossible to tell whether the Russians would be weakened and defeated here.

BEFORE THE OUTBREAK OF WAR (MAPS 2, 3, 5, AND 6)

In line with the general conduct of the war, Panzer Group 3, subordinated to Army Group Centre, was supposed to 'cooperate with the Ninth Army in breaking through the border in the vicinity to the north of Grodno and, by advancing swiftly to the north of Minsk in conjunction with the thrust of Panzer Group 2 from the southwest, to create the condition for the annihilation of the forces between Bialystok and

Minsk'. Its next task would be 'to quickly reach the region near and to the north of Vitebsk in close contact with Panzer Group 2, to prevent the concentration of enemy forces in the area of the upper Dvina, and thus to preserve the freedom of action of Army Group Centre for further operations'.[40] Army Group Centre had put Panzer Group 3 under the control of the Ninth Army for the first breakthrough, and had given it the Molodechno-Lake Naroch line as its initial goal.

I learnt only after the war of Brauchitsch's operational intention of eventually turning the mobile forces of Army Group Centre northwards in support of Army Group North. As the commander of Panzer Group 3 I received neither the Barbarossa directive from the High Command of the Armed Forces (OKW) nor Brauchitsch's deployment orders but rather the orders of Army Group Centre.[41] This was in accordance with Hitler's order from the beginning of January 1940 that each individual was permitted to learn only what was necessary. But there was undoubtedly concern within Army Group Centre that Panzer Group 3 might be directed towards their left neighbour too early. In fact, everyone within Panzer Group 3 was absorbed by the idea of driving on Moscow. However, it can probably be assumed that Brauchitsch, if he had truly wanted to carry out Hitler's wishes, would have informed the field commanders of this intention. Furthermore, the demand of Directive No. 21 for 'bold operations' was not forwarded on by Brauchitsch. He perhaps considered the term 'bold' as unusual and dangerous.

A question of operational significance for the advance of Panzer Group 3 to and over the Neman was whether the fighting for this river should be led by armoured or infantry divisions. In the attack sector were four river crossings. They were 45, 65, and 70 kilometres away from the Reich border. It was of the utmost operational importance to reach and, if possible, to cross the Neman on the first day of the offensive so as to begin the construction of military bridges at night. Only by taking the fixed bridges quickly could they be expected to fall into our hands intact. Panzer Group 3 therefore planned to commit a panzer division to each of the four bridges and for this purpose made every route in the attack zone available to the panzer corps. Both infantry corps of the Ninth Army (V and VI) would follow the panzer corps across the river.

Brauchitsch envisioned the initial breakthrough differently. He feared that the fighting power of the mobile units would be severely weakened even by the opening battles and that the distance of the infantry corps from the armoured spearheads would be too great if they had to remain behind. He therefore pushed for the subordination of the infantry to the panzer corps. They could assemble together at the border and 'advance on secondary roads'. The commander of Panzer Group 4, Colonel-General Erich Hoepner, had straightforwardly described this procedure as 'highly inexpedient'.[42] The commanders of the two other panzer groups also resisted a procedure which had already proved a failure in the West, where the horse-drawn vehicles of the infantry divisions, despite all prohibitions, overcrowded the roads reserved for motorised units. It so happened that the tracked armoured divisions found 'their' routes obstructed by horse-drawn vehicles precisely at the moment of success. At Panzer Group 3 it was evident that the distances to the bridge sites could under no circumstances be covered by infantry divisions in one day, in which case the enemy would find time to establish defences behind the Neman.

In hours of debate Brauchitsch remained determined in his view. Panzer Group 3 made a conciliatory proposal, which would place both of the now subordinated infantry corps on the front line, though would clearly delimit their area of movement from that of the panzer corps. This proposal was approved.

The following was now arranged (see map 3): the LVII Panzer Corps, with two panzer divisions one after another, would move on the bridge at Merkine. The 18th Motorised Infantry Division, as well as some 2000 vehicles belonging to the air force, needed to cross over this bridge.

The V Corps would head from the Suwalki region through Lazdijai towards Seirijai. Accordingly, the Seirijai–Olita road, which was in good condition, was unavailable for mobile units.

The XXXIX Panzer Corps, with both panzer divisions abreast and followed by the 20th and 14th Motorised Infantry Divisions, would advance on Kalvarija and then veer towards Olita.

The VI Corps would proceed through Mariampol towards Prienai.

The operational disadvantages were that both panzer corps could probably only advance over the Neman with one panzer division at a time and that the bridge at Prienai would only be reached on the second day of the attack at the earliest.

In an operational war game that I held with the commanding generals and the commanders of the panzer divisions, it transpired that the spearheads of both corps were dangerously diverted to the right and left by enemy attacks on Lida and Vilnius, and thus the panzer group was split in two. In order to prevent this as far as possible, the LVII Panzer Corps was instructed to have parts of the 18th Motorised Infantry Division follow the leading panzer division over the Neman and to entrust it with the protection of the right flank. In contrast, the seizure of the southern part of Vilnius was necessary for the acquisition of the roads leading through Vilnius to Minsk and further east.

In another war game led by the commander of Army Group Centre, Field-Marshal Fedor von Bock, the question was discussed as to when Panzer Group 3, pushing towards the Western Dvina, would turn to the southeast to drive on Minsk. In March 1941 I had reported the following as my objective: 'to reach the Dokshitzy-Glubokoye-Szarkowszczyzna line with the armoured divisions from where the main part could either turn towards Vitebsk or advance over the Western Dvina on both sides of Polotsk'. This corresponded to the objective of Army Group Centre: 'to advance with Panzer Groups 2 and 3 beyond Minsk on either side to the area around and to the north of Smolensk'. So the encirclement would be completed not at Minsk, as planned in the OKH deployment orders, but rather at Smolensk. This objective was based on the expectation that the enemy forces around Bialystok, in recognition of the threat of envelopment, would quickly withdraw eastwards. In the future it will still be best to follow the advice of Moltke: 'to take the most advantageous scenario for the enemy as a guide for ascertaining the probabilities'.[43] After all, it was at least an eight-day march to cover the distance from Bialystok to Minsk; enemy forces in Minsk would almost certainly withdraw eastwards. The high command of Army Group Centre thus set the Molodechno-Lake Naroch line as the initial goal for Panzer Group 3.

The deployment orders for Panzer Group 3 of 12 March 1941, revised on 24 May, formulated its objective as follows:

> Panzer Group 3, to be subordinated to the high command of the Ninth Army before charging ahead on the left wing of the army group, will force its way through the enemy situated west of the Neman towards Merkine, Olita, and Prienai and will capture these crossings. Without awaiting the rear divisions, the panzer group will conduct a strike against enemy forces presumed to be near Vilnius and will separate them from Minsk. With the aim of outflanking to the north enemy forces near Minsk, the panzer group will advance to the Molodechno-Lake Naroch line, ready to move eastwards in the direction of Borisov. The panzer group will then cooperate with Panzer Group 2, approaching from the southwest, in the annihilation of the forces near Minsk or will continue its manoeuvre of encirclement towards the upper Western Dvina in the direction of Vitebsk and further north.

It may be argued that the objective in this communication to the subordinate commanders was too extensive, contradicting Moltke's declaration that 'no operational plan extends with any certainty beyond the first encounter with the enemy's main strength'.[44] In contrast it can be said that this communication was issued some time before the Russian campaign so that it could be read at leisure. It was primarily for those commanders still without experience in the leadership of mobile units so as to familiarise them with the direction of the operation. Finally, the panzer group planned not to 'encounter the enemy's main strength' but to penetrate by assault through a weakly occupied part of the enemy front.

It was in this sense that the orders to the corps headquarters were issued (see appendix 1a). The LVII Panzer Corps was advised of the need to defend the right flank against Russian forces covering Lida and of the importance of the Oshmyany ridge. The XXXIX Panzer Corps was to attack Vilnius from the south and to hurl the enemy over the Viliya without pursuing them further north.

The deployment orders included a very detailed overview of movements for the strategic concentration and assembly of troops at the border. On 16 June the order for an attack across the Reich frontier was issued (see appendix 1b). This order was necessary so that the findings of regional reconnaissance and the assessment of the enemy could be taken into account, details which had been unavailable when the deployment orders were issued. Finally, Panzer Group 3 issued a 'directive for the conduct of operations', which was essential on the basis of experiences in field manoeuvres and war games, and which was supposed to prepare the troop commanders for the specific conditions of battle in the east (appendix 2).

The mobile units remained concealed for as long as possible, so everything was done to compensate for the drawbacks of their very late arrival in the east. It was impressed on each soldier of the panzer group that the goal of every action was to:

Cross the Neman!
Approach the Western Dvina!

THREE

DESTRUCTION OF THE ENEMY IN THE BORDER AREAS
22 JUNE–1 JULY

PENETRATION TO THE VILNIUS-LIDA ROAD: SURPRISE OF 22 JUNE 1941 (MAP 3)

Shortly after 3 a.m. on 22 June the four corps of the panzer group crossed the border in combat formation covered from behind by the artillery and from the air by the close support group of the VIII Air Corps. Meanwhile, the bombers of the air corps attacked the aerodromes of the Red Air Force in order to eliminate them.

The first day of the attack proceeded completely according to plan, achieving strategic surprise despite the large concentration of troops overnight along the Russo-German border. For Panzer Group 3 there was only one major surprise: all three fixed bridges assigned to the panzer divisions fell intact into German hands. A captured Russian pioneer officer stated that he had been under orders to blow up the bridges in Olita at 7 p.m. By adhering literally to this time he did not have the opportunity to carry out his orders. The LVII Panzer Corps, advancing through densely wooded and lake-rich terrain, encountered several well-defended obstacles which at first severely delayed the tanks of the 12th Panzer Division. Nevertheless, Merkine was taken in the afternoon and the destruction of the Neman bridges prevented. By the evening the panzer regiment was in action at Varena.

Close to the border east of Sejny both divisions of the V Corps had already come across entrenched enemy security detachments that fought to the last despite a lack of artillery support. The Russians time and again resisted tenaciously the advance to the Neman. Nonetheless, an advance detachment of the corps reached and crossed the river between Olita and Merkine.

The XXXIX Panzer Corps had committed both panzer regiments along the Suwalki-Kalvarija road against the threatening heights to the south of Kalvarija and had even drawn on parts of the 20th Motorised Infantry Division. Such strength proved to be unnecessary because the enemy retreated northwards, evacuating these heights and the fortifications on which a construction battalion had worked for three months. German tanks entered Olita by noon and secured the undamaged bridges. Since the following infantry and artillery were delayed, the fighting in the city continued into the evening. The 20th Panzer Division, circling around the north of Kalvarija, also met with resistance in the intermediate terrain, but likewise arrived in Olita in the evening.

The VI Corps ran into strong enemy resistance near Mariampol and only reached the Neman on 23 June, finding the bridge in Prienai destroyed.

South of the panzer group the northern wing of the adjacent unit, the 161st Division, had arrived at the Neman near Druskieniki. The northern adjacent unit, the II Corps, was attacking towards Kovno. North of the Neman, Panzer Group 4 was approaching the valley of the Dubysa. We only learnt later that the viaduct near Ariogala had successfully fallen into the hands of the LVI Panzer Corps on 22 June. There was also no news available regarding Panzer Group 2.

In the evening at the headquarters of Panzer Group 3 (east of Suwalki) we evaluated the position, based on the reports received and on our personal impressions, as follows: The capture of the three fixed bridges over the Neman succeeded due to the utter surprise of the enemy and his consequent disunity of leadership. We encountered parts of the three divisions expected in the Suwalki region. Opposite the northern panzer corps was a Lithuanian corps whose personnel was heavily permeated with Russian officers and commissars. They had hitherto put up a dogged defence. Apparently they were supposed to hold onto the left bank of the Neman. Enemy tanks and planes had not appeared. Aerial reconnaissance in clear weather had detected no movement east of the Neman. According to a captured Lithuanian officer, strong forces ought to be situated near Kovno. The intention of the enemy remained unknown. In such uncertainty could the panzer group push further or should it close the gap around the captured bridgeheads? What would be organised for 23 June?

There was no doubt for the staff of Panzer Group 3 that the advantages of the surprise attack would have to be exploited on the next day with all available strength. The panzer corps had to gain ground far to the east to prevent congestion on the bridges. It would have to be ensured that the bridges were fully utilised day and night to clear the western bank of the Neman. New orders were unnecessary per se. However, the unexpectedly rapid acquisition of the right bank of the Neman had created a new situation. It was particularly important to clear the remnants of the forces believed to be near Vilnius and to make use of every opportunity to capture the major road junction in the city. The XXXIX Panzer Corps therefore received orders to take the southern part of Vilnius on 23 June so that it could then advance on Mikhalishki. Given the uncertainty over the position of the enemy near Vilnius it seemed advisable to avoid bringing the LVII Panzer Corps eastwards over the Lida-Vilnius road, since it may have become necessary for both corps to cooperate to the southwest of Vilnius. However, it was hoped that the LVII Panzer Corps would soon be available to resume its advance on Oshmyany.

Furthermore, we requested the transfer of the V and VI Corps from the command of Panzer Group 3 to that of the army group so as to guarantee the maximum operational use of the panzer group. Meanwhile, technical preparations were being made for the relocation of the command post of the panzer group to the east bank of the Neman in Olita.

23 JUNE 1941: DISAPPOINTMENT (MAP 3)

After the surprising success of the first day of the attack the results of the second day fell short of expectations. This was due neither to the movements of the enemy nor to a failure of our troops and leaders but rather to the scale of unforeseen difficulties presented by the terrain. On this day the motorised units had to pass through the Rudnicka Forest, a sandy, hilly region covered with untouched natural woods that had probably never seen a motor vehicle. All the east-west routes marked on maps as roads turned out to be unmaintained dirt roads which placed almost unbearable demands on our equipment, especially the wheeled vehicles of French manufacture. Vehicles repeatedly became stuck in deep sand or broke down after surmounting a slope, thereby impeding the following march column due to the impossibility of bypassing obstacles on the narrow forest roads. The march column became ever longer, and movement frequently ceased. Since an unfolding of the column could not be considered, even weak enemy resistance at its head caused long standstills. The appearance of scattered parts of the enemy on the flank and to the rear further slowed the advance. Along with the impenetrable clouds of dust, forest fires, whether intentionally started by the enemy or caused in combat, intensified the problems our leadership confronted. The commanders at all levels tirelessly sought to sustain the momentum of the spearhead in order to reach the objectives of the offensive. Infantrymen and artillerymen consistently helped to free bogged-down wheeled vehicles. Small streams bridged by miserable wooden pathways were potentially hazardous, so pioneer troops were needed to make them passable. For the senior leadership, eager to forge ahead, it was an ordeal to witness this thorough suffocation of the 'mobile' units.

In detail, the day ran as follows: Decisive for the operation was the drive on Vilnius by the XXXIX Panzer Corps. Relieved overnight by the infantry, the panzer regiment of the 7th Panzer Division departed Olita in the early morning and came up against the Russian 5th Tank Division approaching from the troop training grounds in Varena. With experience from many tank battles in the Western campaign, the regimental commander, Colonel Karl Rothenburg, reported the annihilation of the enemy division in the 'toughest tank battle to date'. The remnants fled to the northeast and in the next few days lost their last tanks in the Rudnicka Forest. The first determined attempt by the Russians to arrest the German advance had failed. The incoming reports throughout the day revealed that the opposing Lithuanian corps, after its courageous defence on 22 June, now began to disintegrate. The enemy, driven into the forests by the German air force, tried in some places to wage guerrilla warfare against our march columns, albeit without unified leadership. Also, despite consistently good weather, aerial reconnaissance failed to locate troop movements from the east to the Lida-Vilnius line and from Vilnius to the Neman. The enemy presumed to be near Vilnius was tied down by the attack of Army Group North on Kovno and by the advance of Panzer Group 4 on the Viliya. Strong enemy forces to the south of Vilnius were no longer to be expected, so the LVII Panzer Corps was ordered to head towards its original objective, Oshmyany. Rear parts of the corps (the 18th Motorised Infantry Division) would cover the vicinity to the south of Voronovo against forces from Lida.

As this order was given, the spearhead of the LVII Panzer Corps (the 12th Panzer Division) had long yet to reach its intermediate objective, Voronovo. It struggled with similar difficulties to those of the XXXIX Panzer Corps, passing through the southern part of the Rudnicka Forest after routing weak enemy forces near Varena.

There were two factors that particularly hampered the advance of the LVII Panzer Corps. 2000 vehicles of the VIII Air Corps, including heavy trucks loaded with telegraph poles, followed the 19th Panzer Division, which in the early hours of 23 June proceeded through Suwalki and Sejny to the Reich border and then halted along the march route. As the momentum of the forward divisions slowed due to difficulties with the roads, some of the air force vehicles pushed past the stationary 19th Panzer Division and crossed the Neman at the earliest possibility. They very soon bogged down on the deteriorating roads and obstructed the advance of the fighting troops. Other disturbances resulted from the attempt of the V Corps, after it crossed the Neman, to closely follow the mobile units. As it happened, this was useful since there were still many enemy units, unaffected by the armoured thrusts, in the area between the 'tank roads'. So even after a few days an enemy battalion with artillery in the woods behind the frontline was compelled to fight. The high command of the Ninth Army had instructed the corps 'to do everything possible to keep up with Panzer Group 3', for which an advance motorised detachment was established and authorised to use the 'tank roads'. It was inevitable that such movements, beyond the control of the panzer corps, would cause further traffic problems.

Because of these difficulties faced by the onslaught, the spearhead of the LVII Panzer Corps only arrived at Voronovo, on the Lida-Vilnius road, on 23 June. It had thus travelled at least 70 kilometres. The 19th Panzer Division only crossed the Neman early on 24 June and then followed the 18th Motorised Infantry Division.

The XXXIX Panzer Corps also failed to reach its goal for the day. In the afternoon of 23 June parts of the panzer regiment of the 7th Panzer Division exited the Rudnicka Forest and made it to the Lida-Vilnius road only a few kilometres to the south of Vilnius. The commander of the division, Major-General Hans Freiherr von Funck, thought about bypassing Vilnius to capture Mikhalishki. He contemplated entering Vilnius with the panzer regiment alone. The wheeled vehicles of the division lagged far behind. We received no messages from the 20th Panzer Division, operating to the southwest of Vilnius. Machine-gun fire could be heard, but what was happening there was unknown.

Having landed at this time at the command post of the 7th Panzer Division to the south of Vilnius, I made the following decision: The reconnaissance in the direction of Mikhalishki would continue. The Viliya crossing at Niemenczyn, northeast of Vilnius, was to be taken. The attack on the southern part of Vilnius would be executed only after enough of our infantry forces and artillery drew near, if necessary at dawn on 24 June rather than in the darkness of 23 June. I was guided by the consideration that the seizure of the city was only a secondary aim. Sending the panzer regiment there by itself would have weakened the main thrust of the division.

24 JUNE 1941: TRIUMPH AND FURTHER DISAPPOINTMENT (MAP 4)

As a result of the aforementioned difficulties of the advance, on the evening of the second day of the attack significant parts of Panzer Group 3 still remained on the western bank of the Neman. Panzer Group 3 ordered that the vehicles of the VIII Air Corps would have to stop overnight and clear the tank road for the combat troops. We accepted that our aerodromes could not be relocated to the eastern bank of the Neman at this time. This severed the direct line of communications between the air force and the staff of the panzer group, gravely impacting upon air support for the ground troops. A different solution would probably have been needed in the presence of a powerful Russian air force, and indeed the disadvantages were evident in the next few days with increased enemy air activity.

Army Group Centre put Panzer Group 3 under its command and detached the V and VI Corps from the panzer group. It emerged that on 23 June Panzer Group 2 had reached Rozana, 45 kilometres south of Slonim (see map 2), and had pushed further on to Slonim in deep echelon formation. The enemy near Bialystok retreated to Slonim. The northern adjacent unit, the II Corps, had yet to overcome enemy resistance west of Kovno. The southern corps of Panzer Group 4 encountered little opposition against its advance on Ukmerge.

In the woods to the southwest of Vilnius an increasing number of stragglers of the Lithuanian corps surrendered after ridding themselves of their Russian commissars. In the morning of 24 June the LVII Panzer Corps reported that the forward group of the 18th Motorised Infantry

Division was under attack by strong enemy forces to the south of Voronovo, and that the 12th Panzer Division was leaving Voronovo to move on Oshmyany.

The XXXIX Panzer Corps had occupied Vilnius with the 7th Panzer Division in the early hours of the morning after a minor skirmish, and the enemy withdrew across the Viliya. The city was flagged in Lithuanian colours, our troops were jubilantly welcomed, and the panzer regiment of the division then advanced on Mikhalishki. The 20th Panzer Division had reached Vilnius, while the 20th and 14th Motorised Infantry Divisions were on their way there, though their formations extended back to the west of Olita. Early aerial reconnaissance had found no enemy movements from the Western Dvina towards the Minsk-Vilnius line. In contrast, the Novogrudok-Lida road was piled with troops.

WHAT WERE THE CONSIDERATIONS OF THE STAFF OF PANZER GROUP 3 IN THE MORNING OF 24 JUNE? (MAPS 4, 5, AND 6)

The enemy forces around Bialystok began to retreat in order to evade the threat of encirclement, the operational objective of Panzer Groups 2 and 3. On this day Panzer Group 2 made contact with the enemy near Slonim, thereby blocking and preventing Russian use of the Bialystok-Baranovichi-Minsk railway. Enemy forces near Lida attempted to escape northwards. Their urgency to do so intensified in the next few days as the southern corps of the Ninth Army advanced on both sides of Grodno. Consequently, the portion of the 18th Motorised Infantry Division south of Voronovo may have temporarily been in a difficult position. It was crucial to bring up the rear regiment of the division. From an operational perspective, the northward push of the enemy from Lida would surely lead to his ruin if the LVII Panzer Corps persisted with its advance on Molodechno, cutting the Lida-Molodechno-Polotsk railway line.

The threat from Vilnius was eliminated. The objective set by the army group, Molodechno-Lake Naroch, was likely to be achieved by the spearheads of both panzer corps during the course of the day. It then had to be decided whether to move from there against the Russian route of retreat, Minsk-Borisov, or whether to proceed with the encirclement of the enemy by heading in the direction of Vitebsk, or whether to cross the Western Dvina on both sides of Polotsk. The goal of the entire operation, to prevent the enemy from regrouping on the other side of the Dnieper and the Western Dvina, would most effectively be achieved by the rapid occupation of the territory between these two rivers. At the time this necessitated a frontal attack through Glubokoye towards Vitebsk against a presumably weak enemy. On the left flank the advance of the LVI Panzer Corps on Dünaburg provided sufficient protection for the time being. The southern wing could be safeguarded against an enemy retreat northwards through Minsk by bringing up an adequate number of motorised infantry divisions. If the panzer group moved against the Minsk-Borisov line in order to force the enemy still west of the Berezina into battle, Russian reinforcements would inevitably gain time to establish themselves behind the Western Dvina and the Dnieper. Crossing over the Western Dvina on both sides of Polotsk made no sense, because a plan for coordination between Panzer Groups 3 and 4 to the north of the river was lacking.

I therefore reported to the army group that my intention was to bring forward the four panzer divisions to the Dokshitsy-Glubokoye line on 24 June so as to continue with the encirclement of Lida and Minsk by driving on Vitebsk. In the event that this was approved, the necessary orders were prepared. The LVII Panzer Corps was to reinforce the area south of Voronovo (especially with artillery) as soon as possible, seize the Molodechno railway junction, and send both panzer divisions alongside one another over the Viliya through Smorgon towards Dokshitsy. The XXXIX Panzer Corps had to cross the Viliya in Mikhalishki and Niemenczyn and drive with both panzer divisions north of Lake Naroch towards Glubokoye. The 20th and 14th Motorised Infantry Divisions were put on standby near Vilnius for an advance on Voronovo or Oshmyany.

When almost everything was ready a radio message from Army Group Centre was received in which Brauchitsch rejected my proposal.

The panzer group was instructed to veer southeast from the Vilnius vicinity, take the high ground north of Minsk, and cooperate closely with Panzer Group 2 in the encirclement of the enemy retreating before the Fourth and Ninth Armies.

This order came as a blow for the headquarters of Panzer Group 3, which had been ready to shift its command post from Olita to Voronovo. All the efforts of the troops in the last few days, 'charging ahead on the left wing of the army group' to reach the Orsha-Vitebsk line and encircle the enemy, seemed to have been in vain. In our view the main forces of the enemy were still located between Bialystok and Novogrudok. In the coming days he would probably attempt to escape eastwards over the Dnieper, but if he withdrew through Minsk towards Orsha, Panzer Group 3 would need to intercept him at the Orsha-Vitebsk line. Before the Russian campaign, Bock and I had agreed on the idea of an elastic encirclement as opposed to establishing and retaining a rigid line around an enveloped enemy. I therefore made a last attempt to keep the flow of operations directed towards Vitebsk. Attached to the headquarters of the panzer group was an OKH liaison officer, Lieutenant-Colonel Walther von Hünersdorff, directly subordinate to Brauchitsch. The helpful and reasonable Hünersdorff flew to Brauchitsch's headquarters to summarise the position of Panzer Group 3. He reported to Halder, whose opinion differed with that of Bock's and mine. Halder feared that the enemy might escape northwards via Minsk, so he wanted to form an 'outer' ring of mobile units around Minsk in addition to the 'inner' ring (encompassing Novogrudok) created by the infantry of the Fourth and Ninth Armies.[45] Consequently, Brauchitsch's safe yet time-wasting solution remained unaltered: Panzer Group 3 would divert forces from Vilnius-Molodechno-Minsk and form a line of encirclement south of Voronovo-Traby-Rakov-Minsk, including the Minsk-Borisov highway.

THE FIRST ENCIRCLEMENT: MINSK (MAPS 5 AND 6)

Considering the aforementioned entrenched position to the northwest of Minsk, Panzer Group 3 would have preferred to have the XXXIX Panzer Corps strike out to the north of Lake Naroch before circling southwards towards Minsk. However, Army Group Centre insisted that the XXXIX Panzer Corps move along the Vilnius-Molodechno route towards Minsk.

Spearheaded by the 7th Panzer Division, the XXXIX Panzer Corps forged quickly ahead on the Vilnius-Molodechno road. Off the road to the east of Molodechno the division found and penetrated through an unoccupied gap in the line of fortifications. Almost uncontested, it arrived at the highway to the northeast of Minsk on 26 June. Further behind, the 20th Panzer Division had to struggle in heavy combat to break through the occupied line of fortifications along the road. It entered the city of Minsk on 28 June and mopped up scattered Russian forces. The division could not connect with Panzer Group 2, because it soon had to fend off enemy attacks from the south and east.

The sudden diversion of the XXXIX Panzer Corps from Vilnius to Minsk pressed the LVII Panzer Corps southwards to the northern edge of the Naliboki Forest. The reunited 18th Motorised Infantry Division effortlessly repelled enemy attempts to break through to the north on both sides of the Voronovo-Lida road. On 25 June the 19th Panzer Division, advancing via Voronovo-Traby on Minsk, had to fight its way to Traby through hordes of Russian troops now striking towards Survilishki. The right flank of the division was repeatedly attacked with the support of 50-ton tanks. Led by the corps commander, General of Panzer Troops Adolf-Friedrich Kuntzen, the division had to form a wide south-facing front out of the long march column and ward off enemy attacks from the south until 28 June. Also, the 12th Panzer Division, which drove from Oshmyany to Volozhin, pierced the line of encirclement west of Minsk in costly fighting. The 14th Motorised Infantry Division moved into the gap between the two divisions after it had repelled an enemy relief attack north of Molodechno on 27 June.

Whilst Russian attempts to break through to the north from Lida subsided, from 28 June they intensified their efforts against the front to the west of Minsk. The exhausted opponent desperately tried several times to break out, always ending unsuccessfully and usually with the defection of many Russians. These operationally futile breakthroughs could have easily been repulsed by the 18th, 20th, and 14th Motorised Infantry Divisions from the Voronovo-Krevo line and from the north of Minsk (and thus under far more favourable battle conditions), thereby leaving the panzer divisions free to advance eastwards via Dokshitzy-Glubokoye in order to take the Orsha-Vitebsk area ahead of the retreating enemy.

Panzer Group 3 was conducting operations 'with a reversed front', i.e. with its back against still unpacified enemy territory from which relief attacks could be expected. Today it is incomprehensible why the suggestion of the army group to dispatch combat reconnaissance battalions to the Western Dvina had not been accepted, especially since they could have been useful for scouting routes.

Welcome reinforcements arrived in the form of the 900th Motorised Training Brigade. It was put under the command of Panzer Group 3 and entrusted with the security of Vilnius and of the Viliya crossings to the northeast of the city. This made the 20th Motorised Infantry Division available for mopping up stragglers in the region north of Minsk, who had repeatedly, against international law, raided transports evacuating the wounded in the rear of the 7th Panzer Division.

The commandant in Vilnius appointed by the XXXIX Panzer Corps, Lieutenant-Colonel Eberhard Ostman von der Leye, reported that peace prevailed in the city, that shops were open, and that people had resumed work. A provisional Lithuanian government was established which co-operated in good faith with the occupying power and asked for recognition by the German government. It is indicative of the policies Hitler wanted to pursue in the occupied territories that he ordered the dissolution of the provisional government in Vilnius; Lithuanian administrative bodies were to be restricted to the maintenance of order in the city. Consequently, the Lithuanian population was alienated from the German cause.

Once enemy attacks against the west wing of Panzer Group 3 subsided and parts of the Ninth Army approached, the LVII Panzer Corps was ordered to pull out unnecessary elements of the 18th Motorised and 19th Panzer Divisions in preparation for an advance on the Western Dvina. Rather than waiting until the last Russian in the pocket had surrendered, Panzer Group 3 was determined to resume as soon as possible the operation which had come to a standstill against its will. Its daily requests to send the main forces to the northeast were met with the strongest resistance from Brauchitsch, although it became increasingly clear that the enemy had abandoned his attempts to escape to the north. Furthermore, aerial reconnaissance on 26 June revealed the first signs of an accumulation of enemy forces near Orsha. Since 25 June Brauchitsch was pressured by Hitler's anxiety over holding the encirclement of Bialystok-Novogrudok and by the deep aversion of the latter to bold operations. Even on 30 June 1941 Halder expected that the armoured forces would probably only be ready for an advance on the Mogilev-Orsha-Vitebsk-Polotsk line on 5 July.[46]

Attempts by the 7th Panzer Division to cross the Berezina at Borisov and to establish a bridgehead failed due to the firm hold by the enemy of the eastern bank of the river. In the last days of June the division found itself attacked on the western bank by enemy forces from the south. They had broken out of the pocket south of Minsk, apparently yet to be closed by Panzer Group 2. It was therefore beneficial that the commander of Panzer Group 2, Colonel-General Heinz Guderian, landed at the headquarters of Panzer Group 3 in Krevo so as to discuss the continuation of operations.

Panzer Group 2 had forced a crossing over the Bug on both sides of Brest-Litovsk on 22 June. Its two panzer corps swept away the enemy before them, advancing through Slonim and reaching Slutsk and Stolbtsy on 26 June. As the armoured spearheads continued their advance on Bobruisk and Minsk, pressure from enemy troops retreating from Bialystok to Baranovichi had been steadily escalating since 24 June. Rear forces were increasingly required to provide flank protection with a north-facing front. On 29 June the southern corps of Panzer Group 2 reached the Berezina near and to the north of Bobruisk. With a motorised infantry division the northern corps repulsed strong enemy armoured and infantry units along the Stolbtsy-Baranovichi-Slonim line while both panzer divisions of the corps pushed forward as far as Koidanov-Nesvizh.[47] Thus, a gap remained on the east side of the Minsk pocket through which the Russians slipped after their previous attempt to escape northwards.

In our meeting, Guderian and I completely agreed that it was high time for the armoured units to continue the offensive in an easterly direction in order to prevent the formation of a new enemy front behind the Dnieper and Western Dvina. Panzer Group 2, confronting the main pressure of the enemy, had at this time only two divisions in the line of encirclement, while seven divisions had advanced on and partly crossed the Berezina. We agreed that the Minsk-Smolensk highway be allocated to the left wing of Panzer Group 2 whilst Panzer Group 3 could strike out to the north of the Berezina and also complete the encirclement on and to the south of the highway. As a result of these arrangements, the 7th Panzer Division could be assembled west of the Berezina for a northward advance.

On 26 June the southern panzer corps (LVI) of Army Group North had taken intact the bridge in Dünaburg on the Western Dvina, also forcing a crossing upstream from the city on 27 June. The corps had then been ordered to come to a halt, as a result of which it found itself attacked from all sides and unable to exploit the operational gains of its rapid advance. The main forces of Army Group North were still tied down between Kovno and Saule.[48]

While the LVI Panzer Corps had evaded strong enemy forces in its thrust along good roads to the Western Dvina, the northern panzer corps (XLI) of Panzer Group 4 had unfortunately been unable to do the same. Advancing from Tauroggen between both infantry armies, it encountered the Russian 1st Tank Corps as early as 24 June. The encirclement and annihilation of this Russian formation detained the XLI Panzer Corps near Rossitten until 25 June. It resumed its advance on the Western Dvina on 26 June, but by the time it arrived at Jakobstadt early on 28 June the enemy had blown up the bridge over the river, again causing delay.[49]

. . . .

FOUR

AT HITLER'S HEADQUARTERS
26–30 JUNE 1941

(MAPS 1 AND 5)

Not on all sectors of the extensive front had the operations proceeded so smoothly as they had for Army Group Centre, which had received the greatest allocation of strong armoured forces. As expected, it was particularly difficult for Army Group South. The enemy near the border on the northern wing was indeed thrown back by the surprise attack, but he quickly recovered and counterattacked with his reserves and rear tank units, repeatedly bringing the German advance to a standstill. Panzer Group 1, subordinated to the Sixth Army, did not achieve an operational breakthrough until 28 June. Particularly bothersome were heavy counterattacks from the southern edge of the Pripet Marshes against the Lutsk-Rovno-Zhitomir road, diverting strong forces of Panzer Group 1 northwards from their course on Kiev and engaging them in tactical combat. Also, at the end of June the spearheads of the southern panzer corps still stood approximately 100 kilometres west of the Sluch.

Army Group North made no headway in forcing back strong enemy forces west of the Western Dvina (at least twelve rifle divisions reinforced with tanks), although to the rear of these forces Panzer Group 4 had seized the Dünaburg-Jakobstadt line along the river.

The German leadership was now freed from *one* problem which had concerned the OKH before the campaign: the enemy did not consider withdrawing into the 'vast expanse of Russian territory'. His counterattacks halted our advance, and he either avoided envelopment through tough resistance or fought to the last man. A decisive battle had yet to occur. However, Army Group Centre had commenced one of those battles of annihilation rarely seen in the history of warfare. At least twenty enemy divisions went to meet their demise in the Bialystok-Novogrudok pocket. Victory in the Battle of Bialystok-Minsk ensured full operational freedom for the whole of Army Group Centre. The question was how this success could most effectively be exploited. What of Hitler's remark on 30 March 1941 that both panzer groups of Army Group Centre would have to head from Minsk in the direction of Leningrad as soon as possible? Undoubtedly Brauchitsch, and even more so Bock, preferred to march on Moscow. Given recent progress they could be certain that on the way to Moscow strong enemy forces would be encountered and would have to be defeated. But 'the material and moral consequences of every large engagement are so far-reaching that they often create a completely changed situation, a new basis for new measures. Everything depends on correctly interpreting the situation of the moment . . . .'.[50] These words of Moltke are certainly valid today as well as in 1941. What was to be done? 'Of course the commander will never lose sight of his main objective and will remain undeterred by the vicissitudes of events. Nonetheless, the way in which he hopes to attain his objective can never be determined beforehand with any certainty. In the course of the campaign he comes to a number of decisions based on unforeseen situations.'[51]

On 26 June Hitler had contemplated 'transferring the main effort to Army Group South, after the successful encirclement of the enemy near Bialystok, in order to compensate for the current lack of supplies and reinforcements for the army group'.[52] This obviously contradicted the teaching of Moltke: 'never lose sight of the main objective and remain undeterred by the vicissitudes of events'. Hitler then dropped his idea of shifting the main effort, only to readopt it later under completely different circumstances. But on 29 and 30 June, as Guderian and I pressed for the continuation of operations to the east with our panzer groups, Hitler returned to his old idea of reinforcing Army Group North with mobile units in order to take possession of the whole Baltic region, including the Leningrad industrial area. He wanted to neutralise the Russian Baltic fleet as quickly as possible so as to secure German ore imports via the Baltic Sea. He asserted that Army Group North needed reinforcements anyway because the advance on Leningrad would further facilitate the Finnish attack, which could only begin from both sides of Lake Ladoga by 17 July, and would 'free the left flank for the drive on Moscow'.[53] Jodl objected that a detour via Leningrad would exceed the technical capacity of the armoured units.[54] The eventual movement of mobile units of Panzer Group 3 to the north in August and back to Army Group Centre in September placed significant demands on their performance. It is remarkable that Hitler did not impose his own will in these discussions, and no clear decision was made. Yet his military reasons for diverting the panzer group to the north were quite plausible. The final, and necessary, elimination of enemy forces in the Baltic states would resolve the situation on the left flank whilst retaining Moscow as the main goal. The winter assault on Moscow failed predominantly due to the threat to its flanks. Considering the situation on 1 July without foreknowledge of subsequent events, it would have been completely possible on 30 June to order the bulk of Panzer Groups 2 and 3 (i.e. nine panzer divisions) northwards over the Orsha-Vitebsk-Dünaburg line so that they could cooperate with Panzer Group 4 in pushing the enemy back against the Baltic coast. Panzer Group 2 would have probably had to deal with enemy forces near Orsha first, so it would have needed to be assigned some units of Army Group North. It would have been important to commit at least the whole of Panzer Group 3 against Kholm-Lake Ilmen in order to cut off the flow of Russian reinforcements to the Baltic area and to prepare for the drive on Moscow.

A Russian attack westwards over the Dnieper would benefit the

German leadership in its intention to defeat enemy forces still west of the river. Our motorised infantry divisions took advantage of the almost impassable Berezina to delay his advance until the infantry corps of the Second, Fourth, and Ninth Armies had approached. How effective Panzer Group 1 could have been here had it been committed north of the Pripyat! Given enemy superiority in Volhynia it would still have been possible to order Army Group South to entrench itself behind the Styr and to send Panzer Group 1 (or at least its five panzer divisions) through Brest-Litovsk to the southern wing of Army Group Centre. This would admittedly have meant abandoning the ambitious plans in the Ukraine. Although operationally sound, Hitler would hardly have supported this solution.

Later, at the end of August 1941, Hitler complained bitterly that the army, in contrast to Göring's air force, had failed to understand that forces capable of covering large distances were to be used not for the 'self-serving agenda of individual army groups' but solely for the purposes of the highest leadership.[55] It still cannot be proved from the available documents whether this was correct. Nevertheless, at the end of June Hitler refrained from enforcing his will. Presumably he was deceived by the initial successes of Army Group North, especially the rapid capture of Dünaburg.

....

FIVE

FROM MINSK TO THE WESTERN DVINA
1–7 JULY 1941

RENEWAL OF THE OFFENSIVE (MAPS 6 AND 7)

At the headquarters of Panzer Group 3 we were unaware of the vacillation of the highest leadership. Our efforts were directed towards freeing the units that had been stationary for almost a week. On 30 June I reported my intention to withdraw, on 2 July, four divisions no longer necessary for the encirclement of Minsk and to prepare them for the advance on the Western Dvina. The concern that the enemy would exploit the temporary cessation of operations to bring up reinforcements seemed to be confirmed, for on 1 July aerial reconnaissance reported the build-up of enemy troops in the Orsha-Vitebsk-Smolensk region. It appeared as if they intended to move towards the Berezina. No enemy forces were observed to the west of the Western Dvina.

My report of my intentions combined with the concentration of enemy forces between Orsha and Vitebsk persuaded the OKH to approve the commitment of Panzer Groups 2 and 3 against the Mogilev-Orsha-Polotsk line. Hitler demanded that the troops be readied quickly.[56] Army Group Centre ordered an attack over the Vitebsk-Polotsk section of the Western Dvina towards Velizh. The 12th Panzer, 14th Motorised, and 20th Motorised Infantry Divisions would remain south and west of the Minsk pocket. The 900th Motorised Training Brigade would be deployed against Vitebsk.

Since these instructions were consistent with the intentions of Panzer Group 3, my orders for 2 July could be issued immediately. The XXXIX Panzer Corps, skirting the north of the Berezina then driving eastwards, had to take Vitebsk, while the LVII Panzer Corps, advancing west of Lake Naroch, was to seize the Western Dvina crossings in Polotsk.

These orders inspired strong optimism. Given the aerial reconnaissance reports, as well as the fact that Panzer Group 4 had already pierced the Western Dvina line on 26 June and would proceed eastwards on 2 July, Panzer Group 3 no longer anticipated strong resistance on the river and decided to approach it through enemy-free territory on the widest possible front. The Berezina marsh area severely restricted the zone of advance such that it seemed advisable to make use of the more favourable routes to the west and north of Lake Naroch. Any serious defence by the Russians of the obsolete fortifications of Polotsk was unlikely. Retrospectively, we should have concentrated our armoured forces at one point. The 'narrow' Orsha-Vitebsk region, over which the Russians had fought Napoleon in July 1812, was at least 70 kilometres wide, offering sufficient room for three panzer divisions. If these divisions were tasked with the penetration of this region while the motorised infantry divisions covered the Western Dvina between Ula and Polotsk, the chances of success would have been far greater than if the forces, as happened, were distributed across 130 kilometres against two points of attack. This example shows that, due to the threat of area bombardment, modern operational movements require the dispersal of armoured forces to a degree whereby it is still possible for them to reunite upon encountering the enemy. This is the old principle of 'march separately, strike together' in a new form!

The consequences of an incorrect assessment of the enemy became quite apparent when on the day of the resumption of operations a rainy spell began. The armoured troops had hitherto tolerated sand, dust, and heat, but now they had to navigate dirt roads, designed only for horse-drawn carts, transformed into muddy tracks in which heavy motor vehicles became hopelessly stuck. Instead of the hoped-for rapid capture of Vitebsk, the 7th Panzer Division, spearheading the XXXIX Panzer Corps, required two days to reach Lepel, i.e. to cover 90 kilometres. The division was incapable of combat because its march column, constantly disrupted by bogged-down vehicles, had lengthened immeasurably. Further west lay the 20th Panzer Division, which sought to follow the 7th Panzer Division over the same bridge in Lepel. The obvious failure of the newly deployed yet ill-equipped 7th Panzer Division in conducting reconnaissance and issuing appropriate orders, and the neglect of Panzer Group 3 to cover the Western Dvina, gave the Russians their first opportunity for the systematic destruction of bridges.

The LVII Panzer Corps quickly forged ahead on better roads through Kobylniki-Glubokoye and Sventiany-Postavy. In 24 hours the advance guard of the 19th Panzer Division covered the 200-kilometre distance from Vilnius to the Western Dvina via Postavy. Since ground reconnaissance had located a strong enemy presence near Polotsk, the division veered towards Dzisna, further downstream. On 3 July it swept the south bank of stubborn resistance and assembled for a calculated assault over the river against the field fortifications detected on the north bank. On its left flank the enemy retreated before the Sixteenth Army towards the river.[57] On the same day the 18th Motorised Infantry Division was attacked by the Polotsk forces, so it abandoned its attack over the stream running through Farinovo to protect the right flank of the 19th Panzer Division against these forces.

From the line of encirclement around Minsk half of the 14th Motorised Infantry Division was withdrawn and was sent via Molodechno to reinforce the LVII Panzer Corps.

The movements of Panzer Group 2 were also delayed by bad roads and enemy resistance. Most significantly, along the highway near Borisov the Russians launched a powerful attack supported by aircraft and armour against the local bridgehead. It was here that the T-34 tank appeared for the first time. Otherwise, all three panzer corps of Panzer

Group 2 had reached the enemy-held Beresina, with the southern wing crossing the river in the direction of Rogachev. Nonetheless, considerable forces were still required near Minsk.[58]

The southern panzer corps of Army Group North headed towards Opochka (see map 9) where it confronted an old border fortification fiercely defended by the enemy. The northern (XLI) panzer corps, driving on Pskov, encountered enemy fortifications near Ostrov on 3 July. These fortifications were penetrated on 4 July before enemy reinforcements from Pskov could arrive, and fierce battles raged in this area on 5 and 6 July.[59]

Thus, the three panzer groups of the northern wing of the German army were spread along a 750-kilometre front which only extended further as they continued to push to the northeast and the southeast. Panzer Group 3 alone seemed to enjoy operational freedom. The other two panzer groups had to fight for it.

A NEW COMMANDER: 'CLOSE COORDINATION' (MAPS 7 AND 8)

On 3 July the commander of the Fourth Army, Field-Marshal Günther von Kluge, assumed command of Panzer Groups 2 and 3. The Fourth Army was redesignated Fourth Panzer Army, and the infantry corps previously subordinate to Kluge were transferred to the Second Army.[60] On 2 July at the headquarters of Panzer Group 2, southeast of Minsk, Guderian and I had been informed that Kluge intended to have 'close coordination' between both panzer groups for an attack through Smolensk towards Moscow, after which they would press on whatever direction turned out to be most favourable. Panzer Group 2 would force the crossing over the Dnieper in the Rogachev-Orsha sector and would advance with most of its forces along the highway to a line extending from the south of the Yelnya heights to the east of Yartsevo. Panzer Group 3 had to break through the Vitebsk-Dzisna sector of the Western Dvina, overcome the enemy in the Smolensk-Vitebsk region in cooperation with Panzer Group 2, and reach the Beresnevo-Velizh-Nevel line.

During this time Hitler discussed both new and old plans at his headquarters. Again he was indecisive, declaring on 3 July that once the Fourth Panzer Army arrived at Smolensk it would be decided whether it would head northeast towards Leningrad, east towards Moscow, or southeast towards the Sea of Azov. To him it seemed questionable 'whether the tanks could carry out such long-range operations'. If they could, the drive on Moscow might be entrusted to light forces while an advance by the Fourth Panzer Army to the southeast would ensure the destruction of enemy forces in the Ukraine.[61] Seven weeks would elapse before Hitler made a drastic decision.

Based on the instructions of the Fourth Panzer Army received on 2 July, Panzer Group 3 issued 'Group Order No. 10 for 4 and 5 July' (see appendix 3). No defence of the Western Dvina between Vitebsk and Dzisna was anticipated. Along this river and to its east, aerial reconnaissance had only observed minimal eastward movement as well as antiaircraft guns in Vitebsk, Polotsk, and Gorodok. The XXXIX Panzer Corps was to attack over Vitebsk-Ula and, 'without stopping', to take the area around and to the south of Velizh whilst 'guarding the flank against the enemy located in the woodlands surrounding Dobromysli'. Panzer Group 3 counted on the LVII Panzer Corps to force the Western Dvina crossing in Dzisna and to 'advance with the southern wing via Gorodok in order to release the XXXIX Panzer Corps for its push on Vitebsk'.

The instructions of the high command of the Fourth Panzer Army of 2 July deserve attention. The five panzer corps of Army Group Centre were to be committed to an attack over the entire Dnieper-Western Dvina sector, a 360-kilometre front from Rogachev to Dzisna. The proposed 'close coordination' was imaginary. Mutual support between the panzer corps could not be attained in this way. It was necessary to cross two major rivers. We could not assume that they would be undefended. The resistance on the Berezina, especially in Borisov, as well as the destruction of bridges and the resistance of small detachments encountered in the last few days by Panzer Group 3 suggested that the enemy intended to impede the German advance. The current organisation of the

Fourth Panzer Army failed to provide for this. Did it actually count on the enemy fleeing along the entire front? Hitler had already objected to this approach on 3 February 1941 (see page 53).

Was the coordination of forces still possible under the circumstances of 3 July? The expansion of the northern wing through Polotsk out to the north could hardly be undone. The division there was poised for an attack over the Western Dvina, and if it could successfully reach Gorodok it would positively influence the entire operation. The XXIV Panzer Corps, on the southern wing of Panzer Group 2, had hurled the enemy over the Berezina through Bobruisk and pursued him in the direction of Rogachev. It was operationally unnecessary to attack the enemy here beyond the Dnieper. The corps could and should have been used against Mogilev. Only then would Panzer Group 2 have sufficient concentration of forces to drive towards Yelnya-Smolensk. Even a weak man prepared to defend himself can only be knocked down with a clenched fist rather than splayed fingers. Outflanking the enemy behind the Dnieper and disrupting his withdrawal route to the east would have been preferable to attacking frontally. If there was a successful breakthrough between the Dnieper and Western Dvina (i.e. between Orsha and Vitebsk) followed by 'close coordination' of the main forces of the Fourth Panzer Army north of the Dnieper with a view to sending them eastwards over the Smolensk-Velizh-Nevel line, it could be hoped that the Dnieper enemy would be encircled, separated from Russian forces in the Baltics, and beaten in a race to Moscow.

But the orders of both panzer groups overlooked the importance of the Orsha-Vitebsk region. It was vital for Panzer Group 2 to send the strongest possible forces north of the highway for an attack on Senno. Simultaneously, Panzer Group 3 could drive on Vitebsk via Beshenkovichi with at least two panzer divisions. Instead of this, only the 7th Panzer Division faced the strong enemy forces in the Orsha-Vitebsk region because both of the northern panzer divisions of Panzer Group 2 would be committed to an attack to the south of Orsha. Moreover, it was believed within the XXXIX Panzer Corps of Panzer Group 3 that Vitebsk could be taken with just one division. On this occasion there was obviously no recognition on the German side of the need to concentrate forces at an appropriate time and place.

On 3 July it was still hoped that Panzer Group 3 could make up for the time lost at Minsk by taking Vitebsk and the Western Dvina crossing in Dzisna in a surprise attack. However, enemy antiaircraft guns on the river indicated active defence, and the difficult road conditions faced by the XXXIX Panzer Corps prevented a rapid attack on Vitebsk. The panzer group remained uninformed of the offensive defence of the Russians from Polotsk and of anticipated resistance at Dzisna. It would have been wiser to order the XXXIX Panzer Corps to advance to the south of Beshenkovichi in the direction of Vitebsk simultaneously with the northern panzer corps of Panzer Group 2. Then the reins could have been shortened and a nearby objective set. Instead, we believed that we could issue orders two days beforehand. Furthermore, the orders for the LVII Panzer Corps, 'to release the XXXIX Panzer Corps for its push on Vitebsk', were not in accordance with the situation. The 140-kilometre distance between Vitebsk and Dzisna prevented any coordination. Indeed, only after advancing over the Western Dvina and through Gorodok was the LVII Panzer Corps to rendezvous with the XXXIX Panzer Corps.

The orders issued by Panzer Group 3 for 4–5 July are a prime example of the consequences of an incorrect assessment of the situation. Even Brauchitsch was optimistic as operations resumed. Although parts of the 14th Motorised Infantry Division, relieved at Minsk by infantry from the Ninth Army on 3 July, had to be pulled back by the LVII Panzer Corps, the sober-minded Halder remarked in his diary on 3 July: 'I do not exaggerate in saying that the campaign will be won within fourteen days.' He added that it was no longer the enemy forces but rather the enemy economy that would have to be destroyed.[62] This judgement may have been prompted by the great success of the battle of encirclement around Bialystok: four armies with 22 rifle divisions, seven tank divisions, and several mechanical brigades and cavalry divisions were smashed to pieces.[63] Even reports on 4 July of a new formation of enemy

forces near Velikiye Luki and Nevel could not overshadow what we considered a favourable situation.

POWERFUL ENEMY RESISTANCE (MAP 8)

Our progress over the next few days did not meet expectations. At first
all went well. On 4 July, thanks to strong support from the VIII Air
Corps, the 19th Panzer Division crossed the Western Dvina at Dzisna
surprisingly quickly. It established the customary bridgehead in ferrying
operations and thereafter constructed a pontoon bridge which, due to
continuous enemy air attacks, was only completed on 6 July. The infantrymen ferried across the river to the northern bank were almost immediately attacked by strong enemy forces from Polotsk and from the
northwest. Holding out for the next few days against incessant attacks
from enemy ground and air reinforcements, it was only with difficulty
that the division could gradually expand the bridgehead. We could not
consider advancing further in order to make contact with the XXXIX
Panzer Corps; not even as parts of the 14th Motorised Infantry Division,
released from Minsk, arrived on 5 July to reinforce the bridgehead.[64]

After crushing enemy resistance to the west of Lepel and repairing
the local bridge, the XXXIX Panzer Corps initially made rapid progress
with the 7th Panzer Division. Between Beshenkovichi and Vitebsk the
division encountered strong enemy resistance, which it could not break
until 5 July. Approximately three enemy divisions, including two new
tank divisions brought up from Moscow, soon launched a counterattack
which was bloodily repelled by the 7th Panzer Division.

The commander of the XXXIX Panzer Corps, General of Panzer
Troops Rudolf Schmidt, wanted to renew the attack after the 20th Panzer
Division drew near. Informed on the spot about the conditions of the
offensive I expected no success from a renewal of a frontal assault that
had ground to a halt, particularly as the northern flank of Panzer Group
2 (the 18th Panzer Division) was still fighting between Borisov and
Tolochin.

So on 5 July the advance of Panzer Group 3 seemed to have come to a complete standstill. Aside from the enemy group southwest of Vitebsk, five to six fresh enemy divisions behind the Western Dvina were now massed against Polotsk and Dzisna. The 12th Panzer Division was still engaged in the capture of prisoners near Minsk. How could the dead-locked operation get going again? I decided to lead the still-available forces, primarily the 20th Panzer Division, over the Western Dvina be-tween Vitebsk and Polotsk so as to then outflank the enemy southwest of the former. For this purpose the 20th Panzer Division was committed against Ula. I took a hand in the details of issuing orders for the crossing so as to exploit the lessons gained in the West and to prevent the division from becoming lodged in a useless bridgehead. Though tactical-theo-retical in nature, these lessons shall be elucidated here because they il-lustrate the difference in the conduct of battle between infantry divisions and panzer divisions.

RIVER CROSSINGS BY ARMOURED UNITS

Why must an infantry division first establish a 'bridgehead' on the hostile bank before resuming its advance? Normally it is to prepare an attack from the embattled bank and to this end to provide space for the deploy-ment of artillery there. The construction of a military bridge alone would not necessitate such an expanded bridgehead. In this case the crossing troops on the opposite bank, in conjunction with covering detachments on the near side of the river, need only repulse enemy raids against the bridge site. Naturally, divisional artillery requires time to cross to the opposite bank and to move into position in the bridgehead.

It is different with the river crossing of an armoured division. Here too the pioneers need some cover for bridge construction on the oppo-site bank (being held by the crossing troops). Moreover, their task is to clear the bank of enemy mines. Once the bridge is completed the panzer regiment of the division rolls forward over it ahead of the artillery and pushes, without pausing in the bridgehead, in the commanded direction.

Divisional artillery and infantry follow as in any attack.

During the war some leaders suffered from an obsession with bridgeheads. Eventually they were ordered even if no river crossing was planned. This was usually a sign of an aversion to exploiting the strength and mobility of tanks for bold operations. Troop concentrations in confined bridgeheads, especially if lasting for days, are always the best targets for deadly enemy air attacks.

The bridge must be constructed at night in order to minimise pioneer losses and to enable the advance of the panzer regiment at dawn. Consequently, the remaining troops can begin to cross in the afternoon.

According to this procedure the 20th Panzer Division crossed the Western Dvina at Ula. Even though it bogged down in muddy roads on 6 July and was ordered to halt by the panzer group, the losses during the crossing itself were low.

A report I could have given to the commander of the Fourth Panzer Army on the evening of 7 July (maps 8 and 9).

During my return from Ula, where bridge construction had begun, to headquarters in Lepel on the evening of 7 July, I received the following information:

1. Results of aerial reconnaissance:
   Movement of troops towards Gomel via Orel-Bryansk.
   East-west rail traffic on the Rzhev-Velikiye Luki and Vyazma-Vitebsk railways. Movement of small columns from stations in this region in different directions, predominantly to the west. Concentrated antiaircraft guns in Vitebsk, Gorodok, and Polotsk.
2. Radio monitoring took the bearing of a new army headquarters in the area of Orsha.
3. Of Panzer Group 2:
   On 6 July the enemy crossed the Dnieper south of Rogachev

and attacked the southern panzer corps. The attack was brought to a halt. Enemy bridgeheads west of Rogachev and west of Mogilev. In Orsha the enemy was on the west bank of the Dnieper.

At Senno the 17th Panzer Division was attacked by strong forces including several heavy tanks. These forces were stopped. Also, the 18th Panzer Division was in combat at Tolochin. Intention: to force a crossing of the Dnieper on 10 and 11 July with one panzer corps north of Rogachev, one north of Mogilev, and one south of Orsha with the simultaneous withdrawal of combat units on the flanks at Rogachev and Senno.

4. Of the XXXIX Panzer Corps:

    Quiet on the front before the 7th Panzer Division. North of Senno the panzer regiment threw back enemy tanks southwards, disabling four 50-ton tanks in the process. The 20th Motorised Infantry Division reached Lepel early on 8 July. According to a captured officer, parts of a new division from the Urals were at Ula.

5. Of the LVII Panzer Corps:

    Heavy attacks from Polotsk against the Dzisna bridgehead checked.

6. Of the 12th Panzer Division:

    From noon on 8 July ready to advance north of Vitebsk.

7. The high command of the Ninth Army reported that on 10 July the V, VI, and XXIII Corps would reach Dokshitsy, Glubokoye, and Luzhki respectively.

8. Since 7 June Panzer Group 4 was pressing forward in the direction of Leningrad with the LVI Panzer Corps heading to Novgorod via Soltsy and the XLI Panzer Corps to Luga via Pskov.

This information was incomplete, particularly with regard to Panzer Group 2. Had I been aware that the panzer group planned to leave only a defensive battalion north of the highway, I would have reported to Kluge the following (Kluge had arrived in Lepel on the evening of 7 July to attend to the crossing of the 20th Panzer Division over the Western Dvina at dawn on 8 July):

> The enemy position has become clear. The opponent is putting up a fight along the entire front and is now sending divisions from the inner and eastern military districts to the Dnieper and the Western Dvina. In the Orsha-Smolensk-Vitebsk region the assembly of one or two new armies still appears to be in progress. Southwest of Vitebsk the enemy has not exploited his superiority, but endeavours with all his might to regain the right bank of the Western Dvina at Dzisna in order to cover the retreat of his forces before the Sixteenth Army. He seems to be weaker on both sides of Ula.
>
> The aim of the German operation is the destruction of Russian forces brought up for the protection of Moscow. For the encirclement of these forces from the north (via Ostashkov) and south (via Bryansk), the available mobile forces are insufficient; they would find themselves encircled instead. This risk is particularly high in the south, where the enemy possesses full operational freedom due to the lack of progress by Army Group South. It is thus necessary to begin by piercing the front established by the enemy at a point where the cooperation of both panzer groups is possible, i.e. on their adjoining flanks, between Orsha and Vitebsk.
>
> Now Guderian, true to his principle of 'not taking half-measures', has created a strong focal point for the attack across the Dnieper, albeit south of the Orsha-Vitebsk sector. Panzer Group 3 will make the strongest possible forces available to the XXXIX Panzer Corps, entrusted with the attack against this sector towards Vitebsk. Besides the 7th Panzer, 20th Panzer, and 20th Motorised Infantry Divisions, already subordinate to this corps,

the 12th Panzer and 18th Motorised Divisions will also be allocated to it. The attack south of the Western Dvina towards Vitebsk will only be pursued if the effect of the advance on the city north of the river is tangible. It is expected that the 20th Panzer Division will be in possession of Vitebsk by 11 July at the latest, well to the rear of the enemy facing the 7th Panzer Division. The attack of both panzer groups will thus be roughly simultaneous.

It was also considered whether Panzer Group 3 would send the forces from the Dzisna bridgehead towards Ula, but this idea was abandoned. First, the LVII Panzer Corps is tying down enemy forces at the bridgehead. Second, the approaching XXIII Corps must be spared the effort of recapturing the Western Dvina crossing. Third, once operational freedom has been regained the LVII Panzer Corps will provide effective flank cover to the north by heading towards Nevel.

For the continuation of operations after the successful breakthrough it is intended that Panzer Group 3 will penetrate the concentration of enemy troops east of Vitebsk with the XXXIX Panzer Corps. After being relieved by the XXIII Corps north of Dzisna, the LVII Panzer Corps shall break out from the bridgehead to the northeast and shall proceed through Nevel and Velikiye Luki. Since Panzer Group 2 is for tactical reasons withdrawing both panzer divisions located on and north of the highway and employing them south of Orsha for the attack over the Dnieper, Panzer Group 3 must rely on its own strength for the advance north of the upper Dnieper. The Fourth Panzer Army will then be torn into two parts, unable to aid one another, by the Dnieper and probably by strong enemy forces near Smolensk. If Panzer Group 4 then pushes further towards Leningrad, the northern flank of the Fourth Panzer Army would be completely exposed. The relatively weak Panzer Group 3 cannot perform two tasks simultaneously: advancing east and covering the northern flank. The frontal attack of Panzer Group 2 over the Dnieper is not operationally critical. The enemy would do us a favour if he defended the Dnieper tenaciously. Therefore I recommend that Panzer Group 2 limits itself to defence south of Mogilev in favour of leaving a panzer corps north of the highway and sending it north of the Dnieper in conjunction with Panzer Group 3 to the north of Smolensk.

Something like this might have been my report to Kluge if complete information had been provided to Panzer Group 3 at that time. As almost always in the war, only some information was received. Even intelligence on the enemy was available back then, yet the intentions of Panzer Group 2 remained unclear. My assessment of the situation on 7 July 1941 is preserved in fragments and reproduced verbatim in appendix 4.

SIX

THE BATTLE OF SMOLENSK
8–16 JULY

VITEBSK ON FIRE! (MAPS 10, 11, AND 12)

On the afternoon of 7 July the 20th Panzer Division, supported by the VIII Air Corps, had cleared the right bank of the Western Dvina near Ula with minimal losses inflicted on it by the weak enemy. In the evening it had begun construction of a military bridge, and at dawn on 8 July the panzer regiment rolled forward over it to the right bank. The enemy had been reinforced overnight and now resisted fiercely. Only on 9 July could the division, spearheaded by its tanks, begin its march on Vitebsk. It advanced along paved roads, picking up several deserters on the way. The western outskirts of the city were in flames upon the arrival of the division, and in the city centre young communists had set public buildings on fire. Bridges across the Western Dvina were partially destroyed. The resistance in the city was negligible and was mopped up in the course of 10 July. Enemy attacks against the city from the north and the southeast were bloodily repelled. Attacking from the north was a Ukrainian division that had just arrived in Nevel and Gorodok.

The commander of the XXXIX Panzer Corps, General Schmidt, sent the 20th Motorised Infantry Division from Deshenkovichi over the Western Dvina towards Vitebsk, where he wished to place the focal point of the breakthrough. Drawing near to the 20th Panzer Division, the 20th Motorised Infantry Division arrived just in time to ward off the attack by the Ukrainian division.

As ordered, the 18th Motorised Infantry Division disengaged from the enemy at Polotsk and departed southwards. On 9 July it crossed the Western Dvina at Ula and was to strike the rear of the enemy advancing from Gorodok towards Vitebsk.

Resistance before the 7th Panzer Division abated. In contrast, since 8 July the defensive units of Panzer Group 2 north of the Dnieper frequently alerted the XXXIX Panzer Corps of the 'breakthrough' of strong enemy armoured forces. Although these reports turned out to be exaggerated, the offensive activity of the enemy near Orsha still evoked the concern of the High Command of the Fourth Panzer Army and provoked its order on 8 July to Panzer Group 2 to defer the advance over the Dnieper and to seek contact with Panzer Group 3, which was continuing with its attack on Vitebsk from the south.[65] However, Guderian's urgent assertions on 9 July that the attack over the Dnieper would be 'decisive for the outcome of the campaign this year' triumphed over better judgement.[66] On the same day, Kluge approved the attack over the Dnieper. Panzer Group 3 was ordered not to immediately commit the 12th Panzer Division, finally freed from Minsk on 8 July, alongside the 7th Panzer Division against Vitebsk, but to send it through Senno so that it could cover the northern flank of the attack by Panzer Group 2. The enveloping attack of Panzer Group 3 to the north of Smolensk was therefore weakened in favour of the frontal attack by Panzer Group 2. These encroachments by the High Command of the Fourth Panzer Army probably prompted Bock to report to Brauchitsch on 10 July that the interposition of an army headquarters in the issuance of orders to the panzer groups only complicated operations.[67]

The position of the enemy became clearer. According to an order of 8 July found on a Russian antiaircraft officer, the Russian 19th Army with its six divisions from southern Russia would arrive in and to the east of Vitebsk in order to defend the Orsha-Vitebsk sector. The XXXIX

Panzer Corps would smash this formation. Aerial reconnaissance reported that heavy congestion at the railway stations leading from the east towards Smolensk and Nevel had developed because many trains could not be unloaded in a timely manner.[68] In Nevel there was a large assembly point for stragglers to be transported to the front.

Subordinated to Panzer Group 3, the XXIII Corps began to relieve the LVII Panzer Corps in the Dzisna bridgehead on 10 July.

MY ASSESSMENT OF THE SITUATION ON THE EVENING OF 10 JULY (MAPS 9, 10, AND 11)

The crossing of three divisions of the XXXIX Panzer Corps (including the 18th Motorised Infantry Division) over the Western Dvina between Beshenkovichi and Ula as well as the seizure of Vitebsk were decisive. A wide gap was forced open in the Dnieper-Western Dvina front still being set up by the enemy. It was essential to exploit the hereby afforded opportunity for operational manoeuvring in the next few days, but in which direction would this be?

It was tempting to divert parts of the corps to the northwest to roll up the Western Dvina front towards Polotsk and to pave the way for the crossing of the river by the LVII Panzer, VI, and XXIII Corps. This plan appealed to Halder. However, it would split up the forces of the panzer group and would diminish their striking power in the decisive, easterly direction. The Fourth Panzer Army set Beresnevo (60 kilometres northeast of Smolensk), Velizh, and Nevel as objectives for Panzer Group 3. But where would the focal point lie on this arc of almost 90 degrees? If the main thrust of the attack was directed northwards through Nevel it could hopefully strike the rear of the enemy forces either retreating before the southern wing of Army Group North or possibly even standing south of Opochka. But Panzer Group 3 would then end up behind Panzer Group 4 (which was advancing from Ostrov on Leningrad) and to the north of Velikiye Luki in the impassable area south of Lake Ilmen. Since Panzer Group 2 was attacking fiercely over the

Dnieper south of Orsha, the Fourth Panzer Army would be torn in two.

For the purposes of the Fourth Panzer Army it seemed important to keep the enemy forces that had been beaten at Vitebsk at bay and to acquire the ridge between Smolensk and Bely. From here there was a favourable opportunity for cooperation with Panzer Group 2, the left wing of which was assigned Yartsevo, northeast of Smolensk, as its objective by the High Command of the Fourth Panzer Army.[69] If Panzer Group 3 bypassed Smolensk, it could forge ahead unhindered by enemy rear guards and perhaps disrupt their retreat to the east, provided they were not too quickly chased away by Panzer Group 2.

Panzer Group 3 therefore reported on the evening of 10 July its decision to send the XXXIX Panzer Corps northeast through Velizh and the LVII Panzer Corps through Nevel.

The High Command of the Fourth Panzer Army obviously agreed with this decision. It extended the previous march objectives to Dukhovshchina and Milyutina (100 kilometres east of Nevel), though without linking them to the current operational task of Panzer Group 3.

Accordingly, Panzer Group 3 ordered the XXXIX Panzer Corps to the northeast beyond the Liozno-Surazh-Usvyaty line, bypassing Smolensk to the north. The LVII Panzer Corps, in conjunction with the XXIII Corps, had to break open the ring around the Dzisna bridgehead and force its way through Dretun and Nevel in order to establish contact with the northern wing of the XXXIX Panzer Corps. The XXIII Corps, after assisting the LVII Panzer Corps to break out of the bridgehead, was to attack the Polotsk fortress from behind.

As a result of these orders, the situation up until 13 July developed as shown on map 11. Before discussing this in detail, it is necessary to take a look at the world of thought of the supreme command in those days.

AT HITLER'S HEADQUARTERS, 4–7 JULY (MAP 9)

Whilst the mobile formations endeavoured to maintain the flow of operations with no thought other than the relentless pursuit of the enemy in the direction of Moscow, whilst forced marches by the infantry corps partly reduced their distance to the mobile formations, and whilst the principal objective of the deployment orders was almost achieved, the supreme command was still discussing how the operations would continue.

The OKH had received orders requiring that the mobile troops, after routing Russian forces in Belarus, be diverted northwards so as to co-operate with Army Group North in the annihilation of the enemy in the Baltics. The prerequisite for this diversion was fulfilled surprisingly quickly with the encirclement of at least 29 divisions in Bialystok-Novo-grudok-Minsk, albeit with no collapse of Russian resistance on any part of the front. As mentioned (see page 91), Hitler had chosen to await the arrival of the Fourth Panzer Army at Smolensk before deciding whether or not it be sent northwards. This moment was now imminent. A decision had to be made. Once again, on 4 July, Hitler had raised this question in one of his talks in the wake of the great success of Army Group Centre:

> I constantly try to put myself in the enemy's position. Practically, he has already lost the war. It's good that we shattered the Russian armoured and air forces at the outset. The Russians cannot replace them. What should be done after breaking through the Stalin Line? Whether we circle to the north or south will be the most difficult decision of this war. Is it still possible for Army Group South to achieve an effective encirclement?[70]

This talk prompted the chief of the WFSt, Colonel-General Jodl, to urge Brauchitsch by telephone to speak with Hitler about the further conduct of operations. Jodl said that *this* decision would determine the outcome of the war. After crossing the Dnieper-Western Dvina line, should Panzer Group 2 veer to the southeast and Panzer Group 3 to the northeast (see appendix 5)? Meanwhile, at Hitler's headquarters all attention had turned towards Army Group South, which now had some success. On the northern wing on 7 July both panzer corps had penetrated the 'Stalin Line' behind the Sluch, preparing Panzer Group 1 to drive on Berdichev and Zhitomir.[71]

Only on 8 July did Brauchitsch report to Hitler. Halder also attended, and he initially provided a few figures: of 164 known Russian rifle divisions, 89 were destroyed, 46 were fit for action, 18 were on secondary fronts, and the location of the remaining 11 was unknown. Then the conversation turned to the events in the south. Brauchitsch advocated an operation befitting the forces. According to his plan, Panzer Group 1 should exploit the success at Berdichev by turning southwards while protecting the flank against Kiev, thereby preventing an eastward withdrawal of the enemy over the Dnieper, pursuant to the Barbarossa orders. In contrast, Hitler wanted to take Kiev and to commence a large-scale envelopment on the east bank of the Dnieper.

Regarding the main issue, whether the Fourth Panzer Army would peel to the north or south, still no decision was made. Contrary to his previous attitude, Hitler believed that Army Group North could probably carry out the assault on Leningrad with its current forces. He thought that Moscow and Leningrad should be taken not by armoured formations but by the air force. Furthermore, Panzer Group 3 should pause after reaching its deployment objective to provide flank protection against Moscow in case Panzer Group 2 turned to the south.[72]

Little was achieved with this conversation. However, it is noteworthy for two reasons. First, the fighting power of the enemy was optimistically estimated. Thus far the encirclement of large parts of the Russian army had only succeeded in one place. 89 destroyed divisions is an exceedingly high figure. It also seems as if Brauchitsch failed to bargain for reserves still in the interior of the Russian empire. A few weeks later the number of 'identified' Russian units rose to 350.[73]

Second, it is remarkable that Hitler advocated a sweeping envelopment in the south by relatively weak armoured forces. Three weeks later the chief of the OKW, Field-Marshal Wilhelm Keitel, was at the headquarters of Army Group Centre on behalf of Hitler, and he described such a manoeuvre as mistaken. This matter shall be revisited. New orders were not issued. Both central panzer groups were reliant on their own, yet increasingly divergent, operational views.

THE SECOND ENCIRCLEMENT, 11–15 JULY (MAPS 9 AND 11)

On 11 July the closely coordinated five divisions of the northern wing of Panzer Group 2 forced a crossing of the Dnieper and in the next few days headed towards their objectives: Yelnya (80 kilometres southeast of Smolensk) and Yartsevo. South of Orsha the enemy offered such strong resistance that one previously seized bridgehead had to be abandoned. Further south the enemy sought with heavy air strikes to disrupt the crossing of our troops. Until 13 July it could not be clearly judged whether the enemy would retreat further or put up resistance. The latter seemed more likely, since at this time the enemy on the eastern bank of the Dnieper started a large-scale offensive against the southern flank of Panzer Group 2, apparently with the purpose of separating the motorised formations from the following infantry divisions. For this purpose he brought up approximately 20 divisions that now redirected the right wing of Panzer Group 2 (four divisions) southwards form their due-east operational direction.

In the morning of 13 July Hitler's chief adjutant, Colonel Rudolf Schmundt, arrived from the combat area of Panzer Group 2 at the headquarters of Panzer Group 3 northeast of Vitebsk in order to ascertain the state of the mobile formations, which had hitherto borne the brunt of the fighting. Roughly, I explained to him the following:

In the first three weeks of the campaign the troops of Panzer Group 3 suffered heavy losses, although they were no heavier than those in the West. They amount, e.g. for the 19th Panzer and 14th Motorised Infantry Divisions combined, to 163 officers and 3422 men. Physical stress from dust and heat, sleeplessness, and lack of shelter were far greater than in the West, as was the psychological strain from the barrenness and expanse of the land, the condition of the roads and bridges (impacting on the morale of the mobile troops), and the doggedness of the enemy. His forces emerge everywhere to strike back. Nonetheless, the German soldier is convinced of his superiority over the opponent. The Russians still seem to be losing control of the situation. Only in Polotsk is there competent leadership. The tenacious combat style of the Russian soldier is explained not only by his fear of the commissar but also by his ideological conviction. For him the conflict is a civil war in nature. He is threatened by but does not want a return to tsarism. He fights against fascism, which is wiping out the accomplishments of the revolution.

There is no progress on the southern wing of the panzer group in the direction of Smolensk. Moreover, it is operationally inexpedient to push forward here. Rather, the intention of the panzer group is to pierce the weak point of the enemy front through Velizh and Usvyaty in the direction of the headwaters of the Western Dvina so as to bypass his forces near Smolensk. If the enemy continues mining roads and destroying bridges to the same degree as before, the speed of the motor vehicles will no longer be advantageous. The consumption of supplies will outweigh the benefits, so it must be decided whether to await the approach of the infantry divisions. Given that the advance seems to be running smoothly again, every last vehicle is to be assigned to the drive on Moscow.[74]

This report reflects the disappointment which prevailed early on 13 July over the slow advance (only 300 kilometres since the fall of Minsk on 2 July). In contrast, Hitler's delegate had on his arrival spoken with unwarranted optimism of a 'coup de main' by the panzer group.

In the course of 13 July the spearheads of two widely dispersed panzer divisions of the XXXIX Panzer Corps reached Demidov and

Velizh along sandy roads and with low enemy resistance. From Senno, the 12th Panzer Division had to cut its own way through immobilised parts of several tank formations of the Russian 19th Army. In prolonged battles it drew near to the Vitebsk-Smolensk road without pursuing the enemy to the southeast. It was originally supposed to go through Demidov to regain contact with its corps, but Kluge ordered it to attack Smolensk via Liozno and Rudnya 'to maintain communication with Panzer Group 2'. It was thus sidelined from the drive eastwards.

The advance of the 18th Motorised Infantry Division from Ula to Gorodok was delayed by forays against its rear by the Polotsk garrison. At Gorodok the division met only weak enemy forces, which fell back to Nevel. After being relieved by the XXIII Corps on 12 July the main forces of the LVII Panzer Corps (the 19th Panzer and 14th Motorised Infantry Divisions), which had been contained in the Dzisna bridgehead since 4 July, finally succeeded on difficult terrain in forcing open the enemy ring and in regaining mobility. At dawn on 13 July the 19th Panzer Division had commenced its march through Dretun on Nevel. Individual posts, as well as groups of troops defending bridges, were overrun. In Dretun an enemy supply base was captured. A large fuel depot, torched by the Russians, set ablaze a forest through which the route of advance led. Until nightfall the advance proceeded beyond Dretun on ever sandier paths.[75]

On 13 July Panzer Group 3 was confronted by the question of whether to abide by the decision to advance to the headwaters of the Western Dvina. Just two panzer divisions, followed by two motorised infantry divisions, were available for this purpose. The LVII Panzer Corps would only be able to draw near after a few days. Cooperation with Panzer Group 2 could not be guaranteed; it lacked operational freedom due to the powerful enemy assault from Gomel against its southern flank southeast of Mogilev and due to enemy resistance against its frontal advance on the east bank of the Dnieper. The staff of Panzer Group 3 was of the opinion that it would have been better if Panzer Group 2 had abandoned the frontal attack over the Dnieper. The flank attack by the enemy from Gomel would then have been rendered as effective as a puff of air, and both panzer groups of the Fourth Panzer Army could have been united for an advance on Moscow through a region north of the Dnieper momentarily lacking strong enemy forces on account of the destruction of the 19th Army near Vitebsk.

However, the situation developed differently to that expected by Panzer Group 3. There were signs that the enemy did not intend to utilise fully the space of his vast empire as a means of waging war, but that despite his previous losses he did feel strong enough to bring the invasion of his country to a standstill with counterattacks and stubborn defence. As tempting as it was to prise open the gap in the enemy front around the upper Western Dvina and upper Dnieper (i.e. in the temporary vacuum in the Rzhev-Kholm-Toropets region), there were more worthwhile objectives. It was impermissible to chase targets with inadequate forces. The sense of the campaign plan had to be remembered: divide enemy forces and destroy them piecemeal. Here there seemed to be an opportunity to encircle the enemy forces still north of the Dnieper, even though their strength was unknown. In this connection there was the possibility of coaction with Panzer Group 2, which on the order of the Fourth Panzer Army had advanced 'to Yelnya and to the heights east of Yartsevo'.[76]

Thus the decision arose to defer the pursuit of far-reaching goals and to disrupt the eastward retreat of the forces still north of Smolensk. Nobody suspected that this decision would suspend the long-range operations of Panzer Group 3 for several months.

The XXXIX Panzer Corps received orders to send the spearheads of any of its divisions to the highway northeast of Smolensk and to circle to the west so as to enclose the enemy forces around the city. The following divisions were to establish a southward-facing front on both sides of the Smolensk-Demidov road to prevent a northward breakout by the enemy from Smolensk.

In the execution of this order the panzer regiment of the 7th Panzer Division reached Ulkhova Sloboda, northeast of Smolensk, on 15 July.

For the second time in less than three weeks this division stood on the highway and blocked the enemy from his most important line of retreat to the east, this time 270 kilometres closer to Moscow than on 26 June at Borisov. The highway presented a desolate picture of multiple rows of motor vehicles and horse columns that had been shot to pieces. Behind the 7th Panzer Division the 20th Motorised Infantry Division moved up to Demidov, where in the next few days it had to fend off powerful attacks from the south. The 12th Panzer Division had reached Liozno on 14 July and was turning towards Smolensk as ordered. It encountered strong resistance near Rudnya and soon found itself under attack from three sides. Recognising that it was currently unnecessary to push the enemy to the east against the 7th Panzer Division, it stopped advancing and sought contact with the 20th Panzer Division to the north. The 20th Panzer Division, which was to pursue the enemy in the direction of Bely, had been delayed considerably in its advance through Velizh. Plain-clothes members of the Main Intelligence Directorate (GRU) of the Russian general staff had infiltrated Velizh from the outside and set fire to the place. On 14 July the division veered eastwards from its direction of advance on Bely, but on 15 July only one advance detachment reached the Dukhovshchina-Bely road. In front of the division weak enemy forces fled to the east. The road to Moscow still seemed to be unobstructed. However, for the first time there were difficulties in replenishing fuel, consumption of which had increased dramatically. In the vicinity of the LVII Panzer Corps, the 18th Motorised Infantry Division, on its way from Gorodok to Usvyaty in the fulfilment of its task to cover the northern flank of the XXXIX Panzer Corps, once again deflected an enemy strike from the north. On 15 July the spearhead of the division reached Usvyaty.

On 14 July the 19th Panzer Division had hurled back the entrenched enemy blocking its route and had pushed him back to Nevel. On 15 July the division, by committing its panzer regiment, succeeded in surrounding, taking, and mopping up the city in fierce fighting with heavy casualties on both sides. Unaware of the situation in the city, throughout the night the Russians continued to send supply vehicles there from the west. On 16 July, whilst the 19th Panzer Division advanced towards the important railway junction in Velikiye Luki, the 14th Motorised Infantry Division created a broad westward-facing front north and south of Nevel against enemy forces giving ground to the XXIII Corps.

A GAP IN THE ENCIRCLEMENT, 15–18 JULY (MAPS 11, 12, AND 13)

By 15 July it was evident that the thrust by the XXXIX Panzer Corps to the highway east of Smolensk had succeeded. Amalgamated parts of several enemy divisions surged towards Smolensk and its north. Russian formations that had attacked the northern wing of Panzer Group 2 at Orsha on 14 July withdrew on 15 July. Aerial reconnaissance reported on 15 July that the Orsha-Smolensk highway was covered with columns of vehicles moving in rows of four or five alongside one another towards Smolensk. Heavy congestion was expected here, since the 7th Panzer Division had the highway northeast of Smolensk in its grip, thereby foiling all Russian attempts to break out on 16 and 17 July. The next step was to enjoy the fruits of this success and to encircle the enemy conglomeration northwest of Smolensk until the arrival of our infantry. Having failed to escape along the highway, in the next few days the enemy desperately strove to punch through the ring at Demidov and at Rudnya. Unified leadership was lacking. His attempts to break out ran aground, although individual groups penetrated through to the expansive forests northeast of Demidov. From there they conducted combat for several weeks on their own initiative with methods that were against international law.

While the encircled portion of the enemy north of the Dnieper approached their demise, Russian troops facing the northern wing of Panzer Group 2 retreated eastwards. They re-established a front from the heights of Yelnya to Dorogobuzh, where they were absorbed by newly arrived Russian forces seeking to stop the frontal advance of Panzer Group 2.

On the right wing of Panzer Group 2, near Yelnya, the XLVI Panzer Corps had to resist powerful enemy attacks against its front and against both flanks. The two panzer divisions of the corps on the left wing (i.e. of the XLVII Panzer Corps) turned their front to the north to engage enemy forces near the highway. They lay immobile to the south of the Smolensk-Orsha sector of the Dnieper and were involved in costly, operationally useless battles. Interference by Kluge in his concern over the threat to the flank proved to be debilitating, for it held our forces away from the decisive battlefield site east of Smolensk.[77] On 16 July the 29th Motorised Infantry Division entered Smolensk. This success brought the seasoned division well-earned recognition, but was operationally insignificant, since contact with Panzer Group 3 was not thereby made. Rather, a gap in the ring of encirclement remained between Smolensk and Yartsevo. Even after the release of the XLVII Panzer Corps east of Orsha, Panzer Group 2 was unable to make contact with Panzer Group 3 on the highway. Consequently, some Russian forces escaped in the direction of Dorogobuzh. Guderian apparently believed that holding the heights of Yelnya was of greater importance to the development of the eastward offensive than closing the pocket in the combat zone of Panzer Group 2.[78]

SEVEN

CLOSING THE SMOLENSK POCKET
16 JULY–18 AUGUST

NEVEL-VELIKIYE LUKI, 16–22 JULY (MAPS 12 AND 13)

Even after the LVII Panzer Corps regained mobility on 13 July and took Nevel following a rapid advance on 15 July (see page 111), operational interaction between both panzer corps of Panzer Group 3 was absent for the time being. This was because a gap had developed on the boundary between Army Groups Centre and North, i.e. between the XXXIX Panzer Corps, far advanced to the east, and the infantry of the southern wing of Army Group North (Sixteenth Army, II Corps, 12th Division), whose pace was naturally slower. In Brauchitsch's opinion, such a gap would offer the enemy the opportunity to break into the northern flank of Army Group Centre at Velikiye Luki. On 12 July Hitler had already foreseen the possibility of encircling the forces facing the southern wing of the Sixteenth Army by sending the 19th Panzer Division northwards from Dzisna. On the same day Halder also contemplated manoeuvring Panzer Group 3 through Velikiye Luki towards Kholm 'in order to liquidate the enemy group (between twelve and fourteen divisions) opposing the southern wing of Army Group North'.[79] So it was that on 13 July, whilst I grappled with the decision whether to proceed in the direction of Toropets or to turn my southern wing towards Yartsevo (see page 110), Brauchitsch reported to Hitler his preference for sending Panzer Group 3 into the rear of Russian forces facing the southern wing of Army Group North. Hitler agreed: 'Lunging at Moscow and territorial gain are unimportant compared to the annihilation of active forces.'[80] But an order along these lines did not materialise. Bock appealed to Halder in writing and by telephone: 'The chances of taking Moscow are currently most auspicious. Nothing will be achieved at Velikiye Luki.'[81] He could have added that rotating Panzer Group 3 to the north at this time would mean abandoning the encirclement of the enemy at Smolensk. There remained the hope that an approach by the southern wing of the Sixteenth Army towards Nevel would enable the partial disruption of the enemy's eastward retreat from Polotsk and Dzisna. It was inevitable that the opposing views of the supreme command and of Army Group Centre would introduce uncertainty over the movement of troops.

Meanwhile, on 17 and 18 July weak enemy forces attempting to navigate eastwards through the security line of the 14th Motorised Infantry Division south of Nevel had been repelled. An advance by parts of the 19th Panzer Division east of the Nevel-Gorodok road on 16 July interrupted the enemy's march to the southeast. His strength here was estimated at one division. The 19th Panzer Division then received orders to take Velikiye Luki due to reports of considerable railway traffic at its large station. After heavy fighting against enemy infantry and tanks we entered the eastern part of the city on 17 July and intercepted the railway lines. A train laden with tanks rolled into the station from the east. An abundant supply of all types was captured.[82] While the enemy suffered heavy losses in trying to retake the city on 18 July, the High Command of the Fourth Panzer Army, in outrage over the supposedly unauthorised actions of the 19th Panzer Division beyond the zone of Army Group Centre, ordered the division to withdraw. With a heavy heart the brave troops retreated overnight to Nevel, taking with them the wounded and the prisoners. A month later an attack by seven infantry and two panzer divisions would be required to eliminate the 'Velikiye Luki salient' extending far to the west. The 19th Panzer Division would again strike deep into the rear of the enemy, this time from the south and sealing his fate (see page 140).

After the 12th Division had arrived northwest of Nevel on 18 July, the ring around the enemy forces (approximately two divisions) fleeing from the XXIII Corps and from the southern wing of the Sixteenth Army had closed. In a desperate breakthrough attempt on the night of 19–20 July, a large infantry force hurled itself through a weak spot in the front of the 14th Motorised Infantry Division and reached the Nevel-Gorodok road, where it was routed by the 19th Panzer Division on 21 July. The remaining enemy forces northwest of Nevel fell into the hands of the XXIII Corps. The 19th Panzer Division arrived at Velizh on 22 July. In the next few days the 14th Motorised Infantry Division was relieved by the XXIII Corps and was sent through Bayevo so that all parts of Panzer Group 3 were finally reunited for joint action between Smolensk and Bely (see map 13).

RUSSIAN RELIEF ATTACKS AGAINST THE EASTERN AND NORTHERN FRONTS OF PANZER GROUP 3, 18–27 JULY (MAPS 12 AND 13)

As cover against the eastern and northern sides of the Smolensk pocket only parts of the 7th Panzer Division west of Yartsevo and of the 20th Panzer Division at Ustye on the Vop were initially available. Until 18 July only stragglers, leaderless and prone to desertion, were captured, albeit in large numbers. Stray commissars struggled to establish solid formations. From 17 July there were increasingly reports of movements from Vyazma (150 kilometres east of Smolensk) to the west and northwest. A division from the East was transported into Rzhev (120 kilometres north of Vyazma) and then appeared on the Vop. On 19 July uncoordinated attacks began against the 20th Panzer Division on both sides of Ustye on the Vop. It was time to form a stable front here.

From the north, from Bely, powerful enemy forces also proceeded to the southwest and were intercepted by the 18th Motorised Infantry Division, which had been advancing from Usvyaty since 21 July. On the upper Western Dvina, northeast of Velizh, fresh enemy forces emerged (two Caucasian cavalry divisions). On 24 and 25 July they retreated to the north after suffering heavy losses at the hands of the 19th Panzer Division, advancing northwards from Velizh via Kresty. Several deserters surrendered to the division. Under constant aerial bombardment, the division continued its eastward march. On 27 July it was inserted between the 20th Panzer Division and the 18th Motorised Infantry Division to help repel enemy attacks, which were systematically preceded by artillery fire and supported by tanks. With five divisions the enemy repeatedly attacked the eastern front of Panzer Group 3. This front eventually had to be defended by all of the units of the panzer group, including the 900th Motorised Training Brigade. Panzer Group 2, subjected to fierce attacks at Yelnya, was unfavourably placed to close the still-open gap southeast of Smolensk, so the recently freed 20th Motorised Infantry Division advanced southwards across the highway, wheeled to the east and west, and 'closed the gap where Panzer Group 2 was absent' (see appendix 7).[83]

There remains to be pointed out one drawback of advancing the LVII Panzer Corps from Nevel through Velizh-Bayevo. In this direction the corps would be held up behind the left wing of the XXXIX Panzer Corps. From an operational standpoint it would have been better had it proceeded in left echelon formation along the railway from Velikiye Luki to Zapadnaya Dvina. In Nevel on 21 July I discussed this question in detail with the corps commander, General Kuntzen. I was still considering the capture of the important road junction at Bely, and to this end wanted the LVII Panzer Corps to sweep through Velikiye Luki as quickly as possible. Kuntzen asked permission to march through Velizh for the following reasons:

Further east of Velikiye Luki the road connections become worse. Since the departure of the 19th Panzer Division, enemy reinforcements have entered the town from the east. Ousting him from there will take more time than the long-distance march to

Bayevo via Velizh. Finally, having already stormed Velikiye Luki on 17 July only to be ordered to evacuate two days later, sending the 19th Panzer Division through Velizh would spare it from a renewed attack under difficult conditions.

In agreement with these arguments, I ordered the advance of the LVII Panzer Corps through Velizh. Given the increasing strength of Russian attempts from 24 July to relieve Smolensk from the east and northeast, this cautious decision of mine proved to be correct. The plan to take Bely had to be abandoned. All of the forces of Panzer Group 3 were needed to ward off the relief attacks.

THE END OF THE OPERATIONS OF PANZER GROUP 3 AND THE DEVELOPMENT OF THE SITUATION ALONG THE ENTIRE FRONT UNTIL THE END OF JULY (MAPS 13 AND 14)

The encirclement and destruction of a large number of enemy divisions in the Smolensk pocket did not provide Panzer Group 3 with greater operational freedom in an easterly direction as had been the case at Minsk. The initial absence of the LVII Panzer Corps was a factor. Moreover, at Minsk there was no serious Russian attempt to assist the encircled divisions. He was content with building a new line of resistance several hundred kilometres further east, behind the Dnieper and Western Dvina. At Smolensk, however, those formations of ours moving eastwards had already encountered resistance at Yartsevo and on the Vop from enemy units that had escaped the encirclement. Soon, the enemy attacked with reinforcements in order to make contact with the pocket. The vigour with which he attacked foreshadowed the great efforts that would be required of the German army.

Not until the beginning of August was the Smolensk pocket so constricted by the VIII and V Corps that individual panzer divisions could be relieved and allowed time for recovery. At this time I wrote to Bock to give him a picture of the state of the troops (appendix 6). On 4 August

I conveyed the same picture in a meeting with Hitler at the headquarters of Army Group Centre in Borisov.

While Panzer Group 3 was compelled to remain stationary with its front facing Moscow, Panzer Group 2 increasingly had to shift its focus further south from the extensive Smolensk-Yelnya-Mogilev front. The onslaught of the Russians against the Yelnya salient continued. The offensive launched on 13 July by the Russian 21st Army against the southern flank of Army Group Centre had been intercepted southeast of Mogilev by the infantry divisions of the Second Army. However, the Russian 4th Army, which had moved up to Bryansk, penetrated deep into the flank of Panzer Group 2 between Roslavl and Krichev and was only brought to a halt by the infantry corps. Thus, on 30 July the bulk of Panzer Group 2, mixed with infantry divisions, fought against overwhelming odds along the arc running from Khislavichi through Vas'kovo-Yelnya (south of Dorogobuzh) to the southeast of Smolensk. Measures necessary to get out of this predicament drew ever more forces southwards and thereby laid the foundations for what would be a disastrous development.

In the vicinity of Panzer Group 4 the XLI Panzer Corps had breached the former border fortifications at Ostrov in three days of fierce fighting against newly arrived Russian forces (see page 90). The southern panzer corps also exploited this gap. On 7 July Panzer Group 4 was again on the move. Since the 'destruction of enemy forces in the Baltics' was envisaged in the Barbarossa directive as an 'essential task' that had to precede 'the occupation of Leningrad and Kronstadt', it would have been advisable to send the greater part of Panzer Group 4 northwards over the Porkhov-Pskov line with the left wing heading towards Narva so as to cut off the eastward retreat of the enemy, who at that time was fighting west of Lake Peipus against the Eighteenth Army. It later became apparent that had the panzer group advanced northwards it would have found reasonably good roads and much more open terrain. This did not occur despite the fact that the OKH 'deployment orders' had identified 'the prevention of the eastward escape of combat-capable Russian forces from the Baltics' as a 'prerequisite for a further, rapid push in the direction of Leningrad'. Until 8 August several Russian divisions could withdraw unscathed through Narva to the east because Panzer Group 4 continued heading straight for Leningrad.[84] It is unclear whether Hitler's impatience for a political success led to this ill-fated course. Instead of blocking the sector between Narva and Lake Peipus, both panzer corps were to clear a path through the broad, dense woodland between Lake Ilmen and Lake Peipus. The LVI Panzer Corps would proceed from Porkhov through Soltsy towards Novgorod, and the XLI Panzer Corps from Ostrov through Pskov towards Luga. Though facing only weak enemy forces, they made slow progress. It was thanks to the initiative of the commander of the XLI Panzer Corps, General of Panzer Troops Georg-Hans Reinhardt, that on 11 July this formation veered northwest towards more favourable terrain even before reaching Luga.[85] On 13 and 15 July the spearheads of both of its panzer divisions quickly took possession of two bridges over the lower Luga southeast of Narva and defended them against the onslaught of 'three proletarian divisions' from Leningrad.[86] Despite its momentum, Reinhardt's corps came to a costly standstill in the bridgeheads for almost four weeks because the approach of the Eighteenth Army was supposed to be awaited. The westward course of the XLI Panzer Corps further isolated the LVI Panzer Corps, which had reached Soltsy on 15 July. With insufficient flank protection, both divisions were attacked by powerful enemy forces from the south, northeast, and north. They evaded the threat of encirclement by falling back to Dno.[87]

Since mid-July the initiative had gone over to the enemy along the entire northern sector of the Eastern Front. We now turn to Hitler's headquarters in order to examine the operational thinking behind the movements of the three northern German panzer groups since the beginning of July.

Hermann Hoth (right), commander of Panzer Group 3, conferring with Heinz Guderian, commander of Panzer Group 2, in the Soviet Union during the summer of 1941.—*Bundesarchiv, Bild 101I-265-0024-21A, Photog: Vorpahl*

Field Marshal Feder von Bock (left), commander of Army Group Center, in conference with Hoth and General Wolfram Freiherr von Richthofen in summer 1941.—*Bundesarchiv, Bild 101I-265-0047A-34, Photog: Moosdorf*

German panzer troops enjoy a rare pause during the initial stages of Operation Barbarossa.—*Nik Cornish at www.Stavka.org.uk*

Unlike in the West, the panzer divisions encountered a meagre road network once they entered the Soviet Union.—*Nik Cornish at www.Stavka.org.uk*

Field Marshal Günther von Kluge (seated) with General Guderian, perhaps one of the many heated discussions between the two men in summer 1941.—*Bundesarchiv, Bild 183-L19735, photog: Huschke*

The Panzer III began the war with a 37mm main gun, later enhanced to 50mm, which was still not adequate to take on the latest Soviet designs.—*Nik Cornish at www.Stavka.org.uk*

A German panzer division on the move. If highways like this had existed throughout Russia the campaign would have had a different, and quicker, ending.—*Nik Cornish at www.Stavka.org.uk*

The 88mm flak gun, used in an anti-tank role, became one of the most influential weapons of the war.—*Nik Cornish at www.Stavka.org.uk*

Left: During the first onset of winter, cold was not the immediate problem but the intermittent thaws that turned roads into mush.—*Nik Cornish at www.Stavka.org.uk*

Bottom left: Typical of the roads the Germans found in Russia, which were barely tracks and sometimes not even traced on their maps.—*Nik Cornish at www.Stavka.org.uk*

Bottom right: Infantry on both sides of the war caught a ride whenever they could to alleviate the hardship of marching.—*Nik Cornish at www.Stavka.org.uk*

Once winter fully arrived the ground became hard enough to move, but then the freezing temperatures became another problem.—*Nik Cornish at www.Stavka.org.uk*

After his service with Army Group Center, Hoth (center) was named commander of 17th Army, and then 4th Panzer Army, of Army Group South.—*NARA*

EIGHT

MOSCOW, KIEV, OR LENINGRAD

OKW DIRECTIVE NO. 33 OF 19 JULY 1941 (MAP 14)

We recall that since 29 June, when success at Bialystok-Novogrudok became apparent, Hitler considered reinforcing Army Group North with the mobile formations of Army Group Centre. The military reasons he provided for this were plausible. The panzer group assigned to Army Group North could not, on its own, cut off the eastward retreat of Russian forces fighting against the Sixteenth and Eighteenth Armies whilst also absorbing Russian relief attacks from the east. The annihilation of the forces in the Baltics by envelopment from the south rather than by a frontal assault from the west was a precondition for the further advance of Army Group Centre from Smolensk towards Moscow.

Thrice the opportunity presented itself to combine Panzer Groups 2, 3, and 4 for an assault between Lake Ilmen and Lake Peipus while shielding the eastern flank south of the former. These three opportunities were as follows: at the beginning of July after the encirclement of Minsk (see map 6), on 7 July after Panzer Group 2 crossed the Berezina and Panzer Group 3 reached the Vitebsk-Ula-Dzisna line along the Western Dvina, and perhaps on 10 July before Panzer Group 2 attacked over the Dnieper. Of course, similarly to the Rudnicka Forest south of

Vilnius, the terrain to be traversed offered great difficulties for motorised units. South of Lake Ilmen there are wetlands, sandy when dry and marshy when wet, that extend west of the Lovat north of Velikiye Luki and rise to the northeast to the almost impassable, lake-dotted Valdai Hills. In contrast, vast woodland spreads out between Lake Ilmen and Lake Peipus. Though roads run through it, the surroundings hardly offer possibilities for the deployment of armoured units in battle. But where in northern Russia can long stretches favourable for motorised formations be found? It was vital to pass through these particularly difficult areas without a fight, thus at a time when the enemy was still weak. In the first half of July an armoured formation of Panzer Group 4 covered the roughly 300-kilometre distance from Ostrov to the lower Luga in seven days with low enemy resistance.[88] Under such conditions this was a satisfactory performance. At a later stage, the advance between Lake Ilmen and Lake Peipus along the Luga encountered strong enemy forces which could not be forced back against the Baltic Sea. The moment when success could be achieved in the Baltics had passed. Henceforth, the further advance of Army Group Centre towards Moscow was permanently endangered on its northern flank.

It was a peculiarity of Hitler's to overestimate inevitable local crises and to use them as an opportunity to interfere in the conduct of operations. From 29 June until 10 July he did nothing to enforce the original campaign plan of destroying enemy forces in the Baltics before attacking Moscow. However, on 17 July, 'given the situation of Army Group North', he wanted to send Panzer Group 3 to the northeast in the direction of Vyshny Volochyok so that it could 'cut through the Moscow-Leningrad line, cooperate with Army Group North in the annihilation of enemy forces in the north, and encircle Leningrad'.[89] What brought about Hitler's interference? On 15 July a panzer division and a motorised infantry division of Panzer Group 4 were attacked from behind during their isolated advance west of Lake Ilmen and, as easily happens with such thrusts by mobile formations, temporarily became entangled in a difficult position (see page 120). This provoked Hitler's intervention.

But Hitler's wish as pronounced in 'Directive No. 33' (see appendix 8) on 19 July was no longer feasible. Let us recall the situation of Panzer Group 3 at this time. It had encircled the enemy north of Smolensk and had simultaneously repelled early attacks from the east. Some of its forces were in battle at Nevel and at Velikiye Luki. At best, two divisions could be sent on the over 300-kilometre journey, but they would be unable to recover in the case of failure. Directive No. 33 had no influence on the decisions of Panzer Group 3.

Nonetheless, it was no longer on operational grounds that Hitler pressed for the reinforcement of Army Group North. During his visit to the headquarters of the army group on 21 July he emphasised the necessity of bringing about the downfall of Leningrad. 'The city is symbolic of the revolution. The collapse of Bolshevism will follow the fall of Leningrad. In contrast, Moscow is merely a geographical term.'[90] It was the first indication that Hitler sought a decision no longer in the centre but rather on the flanks.

The successful breakthrough of Panzer Group 1 towards Berdichev and Zhitomir at the beginning of July and the arrival of two panzer divisions just west of Kiev on 17 July had inspired Hitler to make far-reaching plans. But Directive No. 33, issued to Brauchitsch on 19 July, conveyed the expectation that Army Group South should first achieve its 'main objective of destroying the enemy 12th and 6th Armies in a converging attack while they are still west of the Dnieper'. The tenacious resistance of the Russian 5th Army near Korosten hindered the advance of the northern wing of Army Group South towards Kiev. Such resistance was to be crushed in cooperation with the southern wing of Army Group Centre. For this purpose, after the cessation of the Battle of Smolensk, Panzer Group 2 and the infantry of the Second Army would annihilate the Russian 21st Army on their southern flank and then strike the rear of the Russian 5th Army. The directive envisaged Panzer Group 2 thereupon attacking to the southeast in order to 'cut through the lines of communication of the 6th and 12th Armies east of the Dnieper'. The rest of Army Group Centre, 'while continuing its advance on Moscow with infantry formations, will cut through the Moscow-Leningrad line with mobile units'.

Army Group North was to resume its advance on Leningrad 'once the Eighteenth Army has made contact with Panzer Group 4 and once the eastern flank is reliably covered by the Sixteenth Army' (see appendix 8).

HITLER ABANDONS THE CAMPAIGN PLAN

Now this was a complete abandonment of the original idea of pushing forward with a strong centre through Smolensk towards Moscow. The 'strong centre' consisting of two panzer groups and three infantry armies shrank to just one infantry army. Both panzer groups, the main striking force of the central sector of the Eastern Front, 'peeled off to the right and left'. This obviously violated the basic principle of striking where the enemy has suffered the most severe setbacks, in this case between Smolensk and Velikiye Luki in the direction of Rzhev.

What caused Hitler's change of mind? Hitler claimed four weeks later that it had been his intention from the beginning to bring Army Group Centre to a stop at the Dnieper.[91] This is untrue. As we have seen, before the invasion of Russia he consistently agreed to the proposal of the OKH for the main thrust to be conducted towards Moscow. During the past few weeks he could have halted Panzer Group 2 at the Dnieper, but he did not do so.

However, there was a profound operational objection to the continuation of the attack on Moscow. Although the enemy in Belarus had been utterly destroyed with unexpected rapidity, neither the Russian troops located south of the Pripyat and west of the Dnieper had been forced back towards the south, nor had the enemy in the Baltics been hurled into the Baltic Sea. Consequently, in its advance on Moscow Army Group Centre was exposed to the danger of being attacked on both flanks. In the south this danger had already eventuated. Dislodging the Russian 21st Army was a necessary prerequisite for proceeding with the advance on Moscow. The attack by the Second Army beyond Gomel to eliminate the Russian 5th Army and even more so that by Panzer Group 2 over the Desna into the rear of the Russian 6th and 12th Armies meant foregoing an operation against Moscow.

Yet did Hitler actually want to attack Moscow? His 'advance on Moscow' as outlined in Directive No. 33 would have quickly come to a standstill. Was the seizure of Moscow still decisive for the outcome of the war? Would it make Stalin ready to sue for peace? These questions cannot be answered without an understanding of the situation on the Russian side at that time. The reason always given hitherto for the attack on Moscow was that only in this way would the enemy be compelled to fight, but this was no longer valid after he revealed that on no front did he seek evasion. Rather, he wanted to bring the German offensive to a halt along the entire front through dogged resistance and powerful coun-terattacks. His tactical aspiration of separating the mobile formations from the following foot soldiers had again failed at Lake Ilmen. The OKH believed that the Russian leadership intended 'to freeze the Ger-man advance into a state of positional warfare'.[92] However, everything was still in a state of flux. Before Directive No. 33 could become a reality, the battle of encirclement near Smolensk had to be concluded.

GLOOM AT THE OKH

Those around Brauchitsch were dissatisfied with the development of the situation in July. On 21 July he was in a subdued mood.[93] On 22 July Halder regarded the prospects of a major victory to be low. From the 'kraal' of Nevel, the creation of which had required so much effort, sub-stantial Russian forces escaped. Velikiye Luki, the significance of which the OKH understood better than Army Group Centre, was once again abandoned. The commander in chief of the air force, Reich Marshal Her-mann Göring, reported to Hitler the escape of 'large enemy columns' from the Smolensk pocket. This was an exaggeration. However, since Panzer Group 2 had received no orders to close the Smolensk pocket by moving to the east of the city, and since the 7th Panzer Division alone could not extend the encirclement southwards over the highway, the possibility did indeed exist that some Russian troops escaped over the Dnieper at night.[94] Though regrettable, this would hardly have been sufficient to diminish what was still a great success had not Hitler meddled daily in operational details. His tendency to decry individual commanders for unavoidable setbacks on the front led to unbearable tension between Hitler and Brauchitsch. The latter suffered especially, but during this time even the more stalwart Halder complained 'that operations disintegrated into particulars and that whole leadership functions were confined to individual orders which were ordinarily the concern of army groups and armies'.[95] Highly offensive was Hitler's admonition of Brauchitsch which included a lecture on the use of armoured formations and which criticised the operations to date. On 23 July Hitler remarked: 'Given the stubborn defence and ruthless expenditure of men by the Russian leadership, an operation with far-reaching goals must be abandoned while he still has reserves at his disposal for counterattacks. In the current situation we must make do with minor envelopments so that the infantry divisions can engage the enemy and relieve our armoured units.'[96]

Hitler's reproof of Brauchitsch was unjustified. He could have been satisfied with the successes of the previous battles of encirclement, and in fact he had even highly awarded Guderian and me for our command of the two panzer groups involved. Objectively, the following can be said in response to Hitler's statements: It was the tenacity with which the Russians held their positions, even when threatened on both flanks, which enabled such encirclements in the east. No leader would pass up such opportunities. Not only were these encirclements costly to the enemy in terms of materiel lost and troops taken prisoner, but they also resulted in a large number of bloody casualties whenever desperate attempts to break out were made once it was too late.

Encirclements can be brought about by sweeping operations or, if necessary, by tactical breakthroughs. In both cases the enveloping forces risk being enveloped themselves. Hitler was incapable of enduring such crises. But what Clausewitz wrote about envelopments will probably remain applicable in future wars: 'We are talking about a complete victory . . . rather than winning a mere battle. Such a victory requires either an enveloping offensive or a battle with a reversed front because both always give the outcome a decisive character.'[97]

SUPPLEMENT TO DIRECTIVE NO. 33 OF
23 JULY AND ITS ANNULMENT (MAP 14)

On 23 July a new order by Hitler descended on the gloom-saturated OKH. This order, the 'Supplement to Directive No. 33', demanded the coordination of Panzer Groups 1 and 2 under the command of the Fourth Panzer Army with the task of capturing the industrial area of Kharkov and driving over the Don towards the Caucasus. The main part of Army Group South had to reach the Don and the Crimea. The adequately equipped left wing of Army Group Centre was to strike the enemy between Smolensk and Moscow and take possession of the latter. Panzer Group 3 would temporarily be made available to Army Group North in order to protect its right flank and encircle Leningrad.[98]

On the day that this order was issued it was still unclear when enemy resistance at Smolensk would abate. Panzer Group 2, presented with the prospect of conquering the Caucasus, had its hands full, fending off attacks by the Russian 21st Army against its southern flank and holding on to the heights of Yelnya. Panzer Group 3, earmarked for the encirclement of Leningrad, was attacked from the north and east while still restraining considerable forces at Smolensk. Yet Army Group Centre, robbed of both of its panzer groups, was supposed to take Moscow!

Because this order was militarily senseless, Brauchitsch approached the chief of the OKW, Field-Marshal Keitel, and requested that it be postponed until the conclusion of the Battle of Smolensk. Keitel rejected this request.[99] Halder thereupon had the view of the army set down in writing. 'The OKH insists upon the continuation of the offensive against

Moscow, as the Russian will defend the approaches to the city to the last man. It is the nerve centre of the governmental apparatus and possesses the most important railway junction. Its capture will tear Russia apart.' However, this communication was not sent because, as stated in a memorandum from 30 July, 'the directive is partially out of date and the OKW is beginning to align itself with the position of the OKH.'[100] At least the OKW and the OKH seemed to have found a way to establish unity in their operational outlook. It was a final attempt to convince Hitler to return to the original campaign plan. An intelligence report on 27 July was supposed to serve the same purpose. The fighting power of the enemy was still estimated at 80 rifle divisions, 13 armoured formations, and two or three cavalry divisions. In addition, there were 25 newly formed divisions, only six of which had a little combat experience.

Located in front of Army Group South were parts and remnants of 73 rifle divisions (fighting power roughly equivalent to 30 divisions), six tank divisions, and two cavalry divisions.

Before Army Group Centre were elements of 46 rifle divisions (fighting power equivalent to 32 divisions) and three tank formations. Furthermore, in front of Moscow there were 10 newly established divisions. Additional reorganised or newly activated units could be expected here.

Facing Army Group North were 30 rifle divisions (strength equivalent to 20 divisions) and 3½ tank divisions. There were also new, reorganised, training, young communist, and factory security units from Leningrad.

The proliferation of new army headquarters, to which a number of divisions were directly subordinated, indicated that available divisions were being bundled together under certain personalities who were making their mark. The fighting spirit of the Russian people remained unbroken. No insurrection against the regime took place.[101]

Closer cooperation between the OKW and the OKH was already evident on 27 July when Jodl advocated a thrust towards Moscow 'not because Moscow is the capital but because it is only there that the enemy can amass considerable forces. It is the active strength of the enemy that must first be destroyed'.[102] This was in line with the thinking of the OKH. Yet Hitler was unyielding: 'The enemy industry must be struck so that the Russians will be unable to rearm. Kharkov is more important than Moscow.'[103] However, on 28 July he apparently recognised the difficult position of Army Group Centre which, attacked frontally and on the flanks, still could not deal with the Smolensk pocket. He remarked to Brauchitsch that he had come to the conclusion that the long-range operations he had ordered five days previously would have to be cancelled due to the need to annihilate the enemy forces in the centre. He therefore ordered the reorganisation of Army Group Centre. The Fourth Panzer Army would be disbanded. Panzer Group 2, reinforced with several infantry corps, was redesignated 'Army Group Guderian' and was placed under the direct command of Army Group Centre.[104] It would 'attack from Krichev to the southwest in the direction of Gomel and crush the enemy forces there in order to rectify the situation on the right flank of Army Group Centre'. The Ninth Army was to remove Panzer Group 3 from the front on the Vop. Panzer Group 3, initially subordinated to the Ninth Army and then to Army Group North, was to 'cover the right flank of Army Group North by advancing to the Valdai Hills and ultimately cutting communications between Moscow and Leningrad'.[105]

These 'considerations' by Hitler deeply encroached upon Bock's authority. They certainly did not entirely meet with the approval of the OKH, but at least they dispensed with the broad goals outlined in the Supplement to Directive No. 33 and so gave Brauchitsch the opportunity to provide the army groups with orders for the continuation of operations. Accordingly, the OKH issued instructions on 28 July. The first part of these instructions provides insight into the assessment of the military situation and the next objectives of the OKH, so is therefore cited verbatim:

The OKH anticipates that upon the achievement of the initial operational goals as specified in the deployment orders the bulk of the active Russian army will have disintegrated. Large reserves of personnel and ruthless expenditure of poorly trained recruits further enable the enemy to doggedly resist our advance in the direction of the Ukraine, Moscow, and Leningrad. Repeated attempts to attack our exposed flanks are to be expected. The formation of a closed defensive front from the Baltic Sea to the Black Sea and the attempt to freeze the German army into positional warfare is likely to be the aim of the Russians for this year. However, the OKH believes that the strength of the Russian military will no longer be sufficient for this purpose. It is the intention of the OKH to exploit every opportunity to isolate groups of enemy forces from the front and to destroy them piecemeal in order to prevent the formation of a continuous front and to gain mobility for further operations. This should create the precondition for the occupation of the most important industrial areas, thereby depriving the enemy of the possibility of materiel rearmament. Long-range operations must be abandoned for the time being.[106]

The intention outlined here, that of annihilating the remaining 'active' parts of the enemy army so that operations could resume, hardly corresponded to Hitler's attitude, for he was increasingly convinced that the moment had come to conduct the war against the economic base of Russia. These contradictory views had yet to come to a head because in relation to the assessment of the situation the OKH orders of 28 July were consistent with the thoughts expressed verbally by Hitler. These orders need not be detailed here, since they were soon superseded by new directives from Hitler.

OKW DIRECTIVE NO. 34 OF 30 JULY 1941: 'REFIT' (MAP 14)

At the end of July the relentless attacks against the southern flank of Army Group Centre and against its front at Yelnya and on the Vop, as well as the emergence of new enemy forces on the northern flank, reinforced for Hitler the realisation that the time had not yet come to initiate expansive operations in the pursuit of economic goals. Besides, the supply situation at the front was becoming difficult, and it was necessary to afford the motorised units the opportunity to repair their severely worn-out equipment. The new OKW Directive No. 34 of 30 July finally overturned Directive No. 33 and its Supplement and ordered a ten-day period for refitting the depleted motorised units of Army Group Centre. Specifically, Hitler issued the following orders to the army:

1. In the northern sector of the Eastern Front the attack is to continue with the main effort between Lake Ilmen and Narva. The goal is to encircle Leningrad and establish contact with the Finns. North of Lake Ilmen this attack shall provide cover along the Volkhov to the northeast. South of Lake Ilmen the attack shall proceed only as far to the northeast as the protection of the right flank of the northern attack requires. Any unused forces are to be transferred to the northern attack wing. The intended thrust by Panzer Group 3 towards the Valdai Hills will not take place until it has been made ready. Instead, the left wing of Army Group Centre will advance only to the extent required to secure the right wing of Army Group North. Estonia is to be mopped up with all of the forces of the Eighteenth Army.
2. Army Group Centre will utilise favourable terrain to go over to the defensive. If necessary, further attacks against the Russian 21st Army may be carried out with a limited objective.
3. Army Group South must continue operations with its own forces. After the annihilation of the 6th and 12th Armies the bridgeheads across the river south of Kiev are to be taken.[107]

This directive contained only individual orders that Brauchitsch could issue. A clear campaign objective was not identified. Thus the whole of July elapsed with deliberations rather than the execution of directives and supplements. No decision was made on how to exploit the undeniably great successes of the first few weeks. It was becoming evident that on political grounds Hitler would cling to the idea of the encirclement of Leningrad. It remained unclear how and by whom the northern flank of the subsequent offensive against Moscow would be covered. However, for the present there was success in convincing Hitler that, instead of the occupation of economically valuable territory, the total destruction of the Russian army was still the operational objective. But given Hitler's mindset there existed the constant danger that he would regress.

It was most important that Hitler's outlook be swayed by the OKW, especially by Jodl, to accord with that of the OKH. For now this seemed to be assured. On 5 August Brauchitsch heard from Hitler's mouth his very own views:

> Current developments will lead to paralysis on the front as in the First World War. Groups of enemy forces must be separated from their front so that we can regain mobility. It is impossible to do everything at once. At the moment there are three tasks:
> 1. Panzer Group 3 must take the Valdai Hills and as a consequence of this action drag forward the left wing of Army Group Centre. It may advance no further east than necessary for the flank protection of Army Group North, and will await an advantageous moment to jump forward in the direction of Moscow along the Volga.
> 2. Army Group Guderian shall settle the situation at Gomel and then turn towards Moscow.
> 3. Army Group South is to dispatch the enemy west of the Dnieper.[108]

Brauchitsch was undoubtedly relieved, but Halder knew that Hitler was 'beating around the bush' with these seemingly encouraging words, for the urgent issue of committing to a campaign objective remained unresolved. Should the Ukraine and the Caucasus be taken on economic grounds or should the enemy army be thoroughly defeated? Halder was suspicious because at the headquarters of Army Group Centre on 4 August Hitler had remarked that Moscow was in third place behind Leningrad and Kharkov in terms of importance (see below). In a discussion with Jodl on 7 August Halder sought to ascertain whether Hitler wanted to defeat enemy forces or to pursue economic goals. Although Jodl avoided a precise answer, Halder gained the impression that 'he just goes along with it'.[109] Nevertheless, both men agreed that the German leadership 'should not operationally pursue tactical pinpricks by the enemy'.

On 4 August Hitler had ordered Guderian and me to the local headquarters of Army Group Centre in Borisov so that we could inform him of the state of the armoured formations. Both of our panzer groups had begun to withdraw particular divisions from the front. The start and end date of the refit of any of these divisions depended upon the time of its withdrawal. Guderian believed that Panzer Group 2 would again be operational by 15 August. I reported 20 August as the earliest date for Panzer Group 3. We both requested the complete replacement of our irreparable tanks with new ones. Hitler rejected this on the grounds of being unable to deprive the occupied territory in the West of armoured formations on account of the threat of enemy landings. Instead, he wanted to allot 400 vehicles to each panzer group—an insufficient substitute. He was vague regarding further objectives: 'The surprisingly rapid progress of Army Groups North and Centre has created an entirely new situation. The transfer of Panzer Group 3 to the north is no longer necessary. Even Army Group South is moving forward. However, the industrial district of Leningrad remains the primary objective. Kharkov is secondary, while Moscow stands only in third place.' Hitler still reserved for himself a final decision.[110]

DEVELOPMENT OF THE SITUATION UNTIL 15 AUGUST 1941 (MAPS 14 AND 15)

Of the contradictory OKW directives and supplements in the second half of July, the order to Army Group Centre to go over to the defensive yet also to eliminate the threat to its right flank remained in force. The right wing of Panzer Group 2, reinforced with two infantry corps, managed to encircle and destroy three to four enemy divisions north of Roslavl in a breakthrough battle of 1–8 August. The most dangerous threat to the right flank was therefore removed, but with operational freedom in the direction of Moscow yet to be achieved, Hitler's insistence on pushing further southeast towards Gomel so as to dispose of the Russian 21st Army was justifiable. Moreover, on 10 and 18 August the High Command of Army Group South pressed for a continuation of the southward attack by the Second Army beyond Gomel towards Chernigov so that the Russian 5th Army would at last be obliged to abandon its resistance to the northern wing of the army group. Though he had been focused on preparing his divisions for the eagerly anticipated operations against Moscow, on 15 August Guderian reluctantly committed the corps on his right wing (the XXIV Panzer Corps), which since 22 June had undergone barely any maintenance, to a southward attack from Krichev.[111]

Until 9 August the panzer corps was relieved by the infantry corps and placed behind the front running from the north of Roslavl to the Dnieper east of Smolensk. Two infantry corps of the Ninth Army penetrated the Smolensk pocket from the west on 3 August and cleared the area by 5 August. Along the line extending from Yartsevo to the southwest of Bely and then to the northeast of Nevel, a solid front was developed behind which both panzer corps of Panzer Group 3 commenced their refit (see page 118). The attempt to advance the northern wing in the direction of Velikiye Luki failed on 2 August due to the tenacious defence by the enemy. Because of the illness of the commander of the Ninth Army (Colonel-General Adolf Strauß), on 5 August I assumed command of the northern wing of Army Group Centre from Yartsevo to Velikiye Luki.

In the sector of Army Group South the successful breakthrough by Panzer Group 1 at the beginning of July (see page 106) had initially failed to progress beyond Belaya Tserkov as a result of showers and enemy counterattacks. But then the panzer corps had renewed their movement in the direction of Uman, striking the rear of the Russian 6th Army. The western one of these corps, northwest of Uman, had driven to the southwest on 22 July and had stopped Russian forces fleeing eastwards from Vinnitsa as the Seventeenth Army approached the city. Between these forces and the Dnieper the other two panzer corps proceeded southwards in order to deny the enemy his southern routes of retreat, particularly via Novoarkhangelsk. On 1 August two panzer corps of Panzer Group 1 formed a westward-facing front near and south of Novoarkhangelsk, while the mountain corps of the Seventeenth Army marched rapidly to the south via Vinnitsa so as to break through the enemy rear guard at Uman and draw near to the Uman-Kirovograd retreat route. Split up into several pockets, two Russian armies came to an end here in exceptionally bloody battles from 3 to 7 August.[112] By 20 August the entire Dnieper bend was in the possession of Army Group South. On 18 August Panzer Group 1 had gained a foothold on the eastern bank of the Dnieper in Zaporozhye. The Seventeenth and Sixth Armies stood along the river south of Kiev. The city itself was firmly defended by the enemy. On 21 August the Russian 5th Army, confronted by the attack of the southern wing of Army Group Centre on Gomel, finally fell back from the marshland west of Korosten to the Dnieper north of Kiev.

The union of the mobile units in the area of Army Group North had still not resulted in a concentrated strike. Of the six divisions previously available to Panzer Group 4, by mid-August there were an SS division located south of Lake Ilmen for tactical purposes and a motorised infantry division (of the LVI Panzer Corps) on the offensive against the Luga sector.

Nonetheless, the XLI Panzer Corps had managed to combine three panzer divisions and a motorised infantry division. Since 8 August it had advanced from the southeast of Narva northwards over the lower Luga. On 14 August the spearheads reached the Krasnogvardeysk-Narva railway and veered east in the direction of Leningrad.[113] In order to build upon its success, the XLI Panzer Corps should now have been reinforced by two motorised infantry divisions from the LVI Panzer Corps. But this was not done.

SUPPLEMENT TO DIRECTIVE NO. 34 OF 12 AUGUST 1941 (MAPS 14 AND 15)

The destruction of the main forces facing Army Group South near Uman raised the expectation that the army group would succeed on its own in crossing the Dnieper and conquering the Ukraine and the Crimea. Therefore, on 10 August the OKW continued to assess the situation as promising:

> The strongest enemy forces stand before Army Group Centre. Their destruction and the capture of Moscow, yet to be achieved, are the overriding objectives on the Eastern Front. From the central sector, it is tempting to pursue operations to the north and south. However, it would be wrong to employ our forces for this purpose, as it would weaken the main thrust of the campaign. Instead, attacks with limited objectives must precede the decisive blow. On the southern flank of Army Group Centre such an attack has already begun. The forces on its northern flank are currently insufficient to defeat the enemy in the vicinity of Velikiye Luki and Toropets. The elements of Panzer Group 3 assembled here must not proceed to the Valdai Hills. The flank operations will still take about 14 days to complete, so the main attack in the direction of Moscow may begin at the end of August. Army Group North, lacking depth in formation and concentration of forces, must plough its way through to the northeast. This will take weeks. On no account must Panzer Group 3 allow itself to be pinned down in the unforgiving terrain of the Valdai Hills.[114]

Hitler did not object to this assessment. He also wanted to prioritise the elimination of the threats to the northern and southern flanks of

Army Group Centre. For this reason, on 12 August a supplement to Directive No. 34 was issued. As a result of the Battle of Uman, Army Group South would be strong enough:

> to force a crossing over the Dnieper, to gain freedom of movement for long-range operations on the other side of the river, and to reach the ambitious operational objectives assigned to it. It shall therefore prevent the construction of a new enemy front behind the river and for this purpose shall establish bridgeheads on the east bank. Army Group Centre is to eliminate the threat to both of its flanks, in particular by seeking to make contact with the southern wing of the Sixteenth Army in the direction of Toropets. In this connection the northern wing of Army Group Centre will be guided so far to the north that Army Group North, freed from its concern over its southern flank, can divert more divisions to its attack front. Only after the complete resolution of the threats to the flanks and the refit of the armoured formations will the stage be set for the attack on a broad front against the enemy forces assembled for the protection of Moscow. The main purpose of the offensive is to deprive the enemy of his governmental, armaments, and communications centre (i.e. Moscow) before the onset of winter.[115]

Upon receiving this directive those at the OKH might have sighed with relief. It appeared to acknowledge their unbroken belief that the decisive battle of the campaign must be sought in the direction of Moscow. There were still at least one and a half months of good weather expected for the preparation and execution of the attack on Moscow. Over approximately the same duration Army Group Centre had already covered the 700-kilometre distance from Suwalki through Minsk-Vitebsk to Smolensk, thoroughly defeating the Russian elite troops in the process. It was not foolhardy to hope now to be able to traverse the 300-kilometre distance from Yartsevo (east of Smolensk) to Moscow in opposition to the significantly weakened enemy, even when bearing in mind our attrition in terms of men (213,000 since 22 June 1941) and equipment.[116]

Another matter was whether Army Group Centre would have sufficient forces to defend both flanks of a wedge extending far to the east towards Moscow. The enemy still held the Valdai Hills, almost impassable for armoured units, so from here he could outflank any advance on Moscow. It was highly doubtful that Army Group North would be capable of attacking between Lake Ilmen and Lake Peipus towards Leningrad whilst simultaneously pushing its southern wing eastwards to the Valdai Hills so as to cover the attack on Moscow. It appeared as if the three panzer groups of the northern half of the German army on the Eastern Front were not enough to perform a pincer movement on Moscow. In view of the main operation, the panzer groups should have been concentrated between Smolensk and Kholm in early July. Instead, they were now distributed between Roslavl and Narva (i.e. across 700 kilometres) without any possibility of operational cooperation. At the very least, there still would have been time to bring together Panzer Groups 3 and 4 for joint action south of the Valdai Hills, admittedly abandoning an encirclement of Leningrad. However, the opposite took place.

PIVOTAL DECISIONS (MAP 15)

While the OKH still cherished hopes that Army Group Centre could commence the decisive thrust on Moscow at the end of August, on the 15th of the month Hitler, again influenced by a local crisis in the area of Army Group North, came to a major decision. He ordered: 'Army Group Centre shall refrain from further attacks in the direction of Moscow. From Panzer Group 3 a panzer corps (one panzer division and two motorised infantry divisions) will be transferred to Army Group North, since its offensive is in danger of crumbling.'[117] What was the reason for this pessimistic appraisal of the situation of Army Group North?

One of the two corps of the Sixteenth Army advancing eastwards to the south of Lake Ilmen (the X Corps) was attacked by far superior Russian forces (eight divisions of the 38th Army) and pushed northwards against the lake. Army Group North put an SS and a motorised infantry division, both of which had previously fought at Luga and near Lake Ilmen, under the command of the LVI Panzer Corps in order to relieve the struggling X Corps. The counterattack began on 19 August and ended with the defeat of the Russian 38th Army, whose surviving troops withdrew to the Valdai Hills.[118] Hitler now demanded the reinforcement of Army Group North with the mobile units of Army Group Centre, something he had originally intended for early July but had failed to order. At that time, sending Panzer Group 3 over the Western Dvina towards Luga or Pskov would have permitted Army Group North to push enemy forces against the Baltic Sea and therefore would have been a decisive turning point in the course of the operations. Now, six weeks later, Army Group Centre was reduced by half a panzer group at a moment when it was about to take the last step towards Moscow, the operational objective. Instead of being employed at the crisis site, the corps released by Panzer Group 3 (the XXXIX Panzer Corps with the 12th Panzer, 18th Motorised, and 20th Motorised Infantry Divisions) swept in a wide arc through Vilnius to the northern wing of Army Group North. Its task was to fulfil Hitler's desire for the conquest of the industrial district of Leningrad and for the isolation of this 'stronghold of Bolshevism' from Moscow. South of Leningrad, the corps drove far to the east and, with a tremendous effort and with some troops on foot, arrived at Tikhvin. The XLI Panzer Corps had been successfully advancing on Leningrad, but a few weeks later, at the moment when the city appeared to be within striking distance, it had to cease its attack and double back. This corps was allocated to Panzer Group 3 for the eventual attack on Moscow in early October. It was difficult 'to make head or tail of this chopping and changing'.[119]

A few days after the departure of the XXXIX Panzer Corps for Army Group North, the other corps of Panzer Group 3 (the LVII Panzer

Corps) was assigned the task of breaking through the enemy army concentrated near Velikiye Luki with the 19th and 20th Panzer Divisions and of annihilating this army in conjunction with the infantry divisions. This task was accomplished expeditiously from 22 to 27 August. In its pursuit of the enemy along sodden roads, the corps reached the Western Dvina east of Toropets on 1 September. Then it was 'temporarily' placed under the command of the Sixteenth Army. In heavy fighting near Demyansk and between Kholm and Ostashkov throughout September, the LVII Panzer Corps struggled alongside with the LVI Panzer Corps to push the southern wing of Army Group North eastwards to the Valdai Hills. Persistent rainfall transformed the loam soil of the Valdai Hills into mud and thereby made this densely wooded, lake-dotted, albeit poorly networked region unsuitable for the use of armoured formations at this time of year. Therefore, the operational value of the subordination of the LVII Panzer Corps to the Sixteenth Army was low compared with its heavy losses in men and vehicles. The enemy remained in possession of the Valdai Hills. Severely battered, the corps reached Smolensk, 400 kilometres to the south, in early October so that it could join the southern wing of the Fourth Army and partake in the offensive by Army Group Centre against Moscow.[120]

We have rushed on ahead in describing these events so as to demonstrate the impact of Hitler's order on 15 August. The transfer of five mobile formations of Panzer Group 3 to the north in conjunction with the commitment of most of Panzer Group 2 in a southerly direction towards Gomel deprived Army Group Centre of the chance to advance on Moscow. It was *the* decisive order of the eastern campaign, one that Hitler had already announced on 4 July but had repeatedly postponed.

Now, however, time was pressing. For after the execution of the secondary operations, would the autumn be too far advanced to dare still to march on Moscow? More importantly, given the wear and tear affecting our motorised formations, only partially remedied and bound to worsen in the deteriorating Russian weather, would the final decisive blow against the enemy capital still be possible?

These were questions that had been debated in earnest at the OKW and OKH. The OKW 'Assessment of the Situation in the East' on 18 August concluded that: 'The German army in the east is strong enough for Army Groups North and South to accomplish their tasks at the same time as Army Group Centre conducts its decisive thrust on Moscow. It is necessary to forego the pursuit of enticing partial victories (e.g. the southward attack by Panzer Group 2) and to put up with local crises.'

KIEV, NOT MOSCOW, 18-22 AUGUST 1941 (MAP 15)

Despite the transfer of forces to Army Group North, the OKH advocated an attack in the direction of Moscow. The enemy sought a decisive battle on the road to the capital, for it was here that he assembled the strongest forces. 42 rifle divisions stood before Moscow, and a further 20 divisions made preparations in the city. On 18 August the OKH submitted its plan to Hitler detailing its objectives for the attack on Moscow in order to compel him to make a decision. The plan proposed that Army Group Centre would have at its disposal 42 infantry divisions and 12 mobile units. They would be organised as follows:

(a) *Attack Group South*, consisting of Panzer Group 2 and the Second Army (nine infantry divisions, a cavalry division, and eight motorised formations), would attack over the Bryansk-Roslavl line towards Kaluga with the right wing in contact with the Oka.

(b) *Defensive Group Centre*: the Fourth Army (ten divisions along the Roslavl-Yartsevo line).

(c) *Attack Group North*: the Ninth Army and Panzer Group 3 (13 infantry divisions and four motorised formations). Half of these forces would advance from the vicinity south of Bely, and the other half from the Toropets region with the left wing in contact with the Volga.

The OKH set two requirements for this operation:

(a) The ongoing offensive against Gomel should only continue southwards to the extent that it could still turn east, i.e. the infantry should proceed no further than Gomel-Starodub, and the mobile formations no further than Novgorod and to its east.

(b) Panzer Group 3 should not be drawn northeast of Torpets into the battles of the southern wing of Army Group North.[121]

Hitler was bound to disagree with these two conditions. For the time being he was determined, in addition to encircling Leningrad, to place the focal point of the operations with Army Group South. But it was also questionable whether the four mobile formations intended for Attack Group North would have been enough for the breakthrough and for the subsequent operation, the more so as a unified leadership was near impossible with such a far-flung distribution. Indeed, the distribution of the nine mobile formations of Army Group North across a large area had come home to roost because they were now immobilised without any role in the main operation.

Despite his order on 12 August that Moscow be captured before the onset of winter, Hitler's brusque dismissal of the OKH proposal on 20 August finally revealed his disagreement not only with Brauchitsch but also with his OKW advisers. He indicated an operational goal that he had mentioned, and dropped, as a possibility several times previously. The most important objectives for the upcoming operations were not Moscow and the forces that would be encountered on the way there, but 'the seizure of the Crimea, the acquisition of the industrial and coal region of the Donets Basin, and the amputation of the Caucasus oil fields'.[122]

Hitler thus prioritised economic objectives over his previously expressed view of 'wiping out wherever possible the active strength of the enemy'. Yet Russian fighting power in the field remained unbroken, as proven by the ongoing attacks against the front of Army Group Centre, so it was premature to think about appropriating economic resources with which the enemy armed his reorganised and newly activated units. This situation reconfirmed Clausewitz's belief 'that it is no great feat to have devised a good operational plan. The great difficulty consists in remaining faithful throughout its execution to the basic principles we lay down for ourselves'.[123] Hitler's decision violated the principle that the destruction of the Russian field army must precede economic and political war aims. In an order on 21 August 1941 he justified the shift in focus from the central sector to the southern sector of the front by stating 'that such a rare, operationally favourable situation, which arose as a result of the attainment of the Gomel-Pochep line, must be exploited immediately in a converging operation with the inner wings of Army Groups Centre and South'. As a matter of fact, the operation conducted in accordance with this order resulted not only in the annihilation of the Russian 5th Army, as planned, but also in the encirclement of another three armies in the Kiev-Cherkasy-Romny region. It was the largest-scale envelopment operation of the war to date. However, despite its success, within the framework of the German campaign plan it was a secondary operation that devoured precious time and resources, and seriously jeopardised, if not precluded, the capture of Moscow, the original operational goal.

....

NINE

THE OPERATIONS OF THE
BATTLE OF VYAZMA

STRATEGIC BACKGROUND (MAP 15)

The large encirclement of the Battle of Kiev took up the whole of September. It ended on 26 September southeast of Kiev with the surrender of the constricted remnants of the Russian 5th, 26th, 37th, and 38th Armies. It tore open the enemy front before Army Group South. However, it remained questionable whether there was still sufficient time for the achievement of the political-economic objectives in Hitler's order of 21 August 1941, i.e. 'the seizure of the Crimea, the acquisition of the industrial and coal region of the Donets Basin, and the amputation of the Caucasus oil fields'. In southern Russia the greatest threat to the continuation of operations was not the coming winter but rather the present autumn during which rainfall caused the river banks to overflow and made all roads useless for heavy vehicles. It was too late by the time the German leadership became aware of the effects of this Russian 'mud period', which arrived as early as mid-October. Yet despite the challenges of the natural environment, the strategic objectives in the south had been substantially achieved. By mid-November the Crimea, except for Sevastopol, was occupied by the Eleventh Army, eliminating the peninsula as an 'aircraft carrier' from which the Russians could raid the Romanian oil fields. Since the beginning of November the First Panzer Army and the Seventeenth Army held Stalino, Artemovsk, and Slavyansk, the main industrial cities of the Donets Basin. The Sixth Army took Kharkov at the end of October. The oil supply from the Caucasus remained undisturbed.

At the urging of Army Group South a considerable portion of Army Group Centre, namely the Second Army and Panzer Group 2, had driven far south of the Desna during the Battle of Kiev. Two-thirds of Panzer Group 2 defended an eastward-facing front southeast of the Romny-Glukhov-Novgorod line against relief attacks by enemy reinforcements.

The enemy strengthened his position along the rest of the front of Army Group Centre, composed of the Fourth and Ninth Armies with parts of Panzer Groups 2 and 3. This front extended from Pochep through Roslavl, Yelnya, and Yartsevo to the east of Toropets.

Army Group North had closed in on Leningrad with the Eighteenth Army. The XXXIX Panzer Corps, after its transfer from Panzer Group 3 in mid-August, captured Schlisselburg in early September and severed the connection with Moscow. The assault over the Volkhov at the beginning of October resulted in the seizure of Tikhvin, though it failed to establish contact with the Finns, who in early September had reached the Svir east of Lake Ladoga. The corps of the Sixteenth Army southeast of Lake Ilmen lingered on the western slopes of the Valdai Hills.

While the operations east of Kiev were still in progress, there was a revival of the idea of a thrust by Army Group Centre against the enemy forces assembled to protect Moscow. The army group would require the assistance of the Second Army and of Panzer Group 2, but their unavailability until the end of September meant that the attack could only begin in early October. At this late stage the possibility of reaching Moscow was doubtful. Army Group Centre therefore set itself a relatively limited objective. An attack group would pierce the front at Roslavl, advance northeast on Vyazma, and join hands with a northern attack group approaching the city from the northwest. Enemy forces east of Smolensk would thereby be encircled and, under pressure from the rest of the army group, destroyed.

Although Army Group Centre had desired the involvement of Panzer Group 2 and of the Second Army in the attack on Moscow, and although the OKH August plan had envisaged an advance by these formations (Attack Group South) through Bryansk towards Kaluga (see page 141), the thrust by Panzer Group 2 to the south of Romny meant that it had to attack from the Glukhov area towards Orel and strike the rear of the enemy forces that the Second Army would pin down along the Novgorod-Bryansk front. The five panzer divisions and four and a half motorised infantry divisions of Panzer Group 2 had to be omitted from what was now the main attack on Vyazma. Their subsequent advance on Tula rather than Kaluga resulted in the absence of operational interaction between the three panzer groups.

Panzer Group 4 was transferred to Army Group Centre in September. It could have combined both of its panzer corps (the LVI from south of Lake Ilmen and the XLI from Leningrad) most easily at the closest point, i.e. behind the upper Western Dvina near Toropets and Kholm. Then they would have been favourably placed for the army group to advance its left wing towards Rzhev. However, there was little time for an attack on Rzhev, so the headquarters staff of Panzer Group 4 had to take over command of the southern attack group which was concentrated near Roslavl and which consisted of elements of Panzer Group 2 as well as of two panzer divisions of the army reserve. This attack group would also incorporate the LVII Panzer Corps, which was still fighting near the Valdai Hills under the Sixteenth Army in late September. Both the XLI Panzer Corps with its three divisions and the LVI Panzer Corps were subordinated to Panzer Group 3, the northern attack group.

So there were significant forces allocated to Army Group Centre for the thrust on Moscow. In addition to three infantry armies, there were three panzer groups consisting of thirteen panzer divisions, eight motorised infantry divisions, the Infantry Regiment Großdeutschland, and the 900th Motorised Training Brigade. Also, numerous assault guns and medium artillery, mainly from Army Group North, were moved to the decisive front. Two air fleets would support the attack. Thus, everything was done to develop an effective concentration of forces, although it was impossible to foresee the state of the weather at this time of year and how it might affect subsequent operations. Could dry weather, ideal for rapid movement and supply over long distances, still be expected in October? After the Second Schleswig War in 1864 Moltke had written: 'Operations can be based on the season but not on the weather.'[124] The difficulties on the roads in September 1941 showed that the summer had ended completely. Nevertheless, the German leadership ventured the attack in the hope of a decisive victory.

THE SITUATION OF PANZER GROUP 3 IN SEPTEMBER 1941 (MAP 16)

Until the last days of August the enemy persistently tried to recapture Smolensk. The Fourth Army had to vacate the Yelnya salient. Then the enemy dug himself in. North of the Smolensk-Vyazma highway the enemy positions extended from Yartsevo, west of the Vop, to the Novo-selki-Bely road. From here the front bended sharply to the west and then ran along the western edge of the vast marshland which spread out to the south of the railway track between Zapadnaya Dvina and Mostovaya. The front reached the Western Dvina in Bayevo, from where it went further north along the eastern bank of the river to the western edge of the Valdai Hills. At the beginning of September the 19th Panzer Division seized a small bridgehead in Andreapol and, supported by the XXIII Corps, held it against repeated Russian attacks. Even so, the enemy had a well-developed system of trenches and fortifications behind which he intended to spend the winter. A rear line of defence behind the upper Dnieper, round Sychyovka, and west of Rzhev was under construction. However, the actual Moscow defensive line ran from Kaluga towards Kalinin via Borodino, the site of the 1812 Franco-Russian clash. Hundreds of thousands of Muscovite factory workers, utilising all available means of the art of modern fortification, were in the act of building a defensive system in depth, the central part of which was already finished and lay on both sides of the Smolensk-Moscow highway. It comprised concrete bunkers and pillboxes secured by wire entanglements, mine-fields, and antitank ditches. There was no sign whatsoever that the enemy would retreat behind the Dnieper in the event of an attack. The Dnieper line was unoccupied. In contrast, twelve reserve divisions were activated in Moscow.

German troops were positioned as follows: the VIII and V Corps (eight infantry divisions) secured the Yartsevo-Novoselki sector, the VI Corps (three infantry divisions) covered the Novoselki-Bayevo sector, and the XXIII Corps (also with three infantry divisions) stood behind the Western Dvina from Bayevo to the north of Andreapol.

The panzer corps originally belonging to Panzer Group 3 had, as previously mentioned (see page 139), been successively dispatched to Army Group North. The 7th Panzer Division, 14th Motorised Infantry Division, and 900th Motorised Training Brigade were all busy with the repair of their vehicles behind the front of the Ninth Army, though they repeatedly had to come to the aid of the infantry divisions in conducting defensive combat. Casualties, especially amongst junior officers, were higher than in the preceding offensive engagements. They were only partially replaced. Furthermore, the supply of new engines and tanks was insufficient to bring the divisions up to full combat strength.

OPERATIONAL CONSIDERATIONS

At the beginning of September Bock requested from me an operational outline based on the following idea: the Ninth Army had to break through opposing enemy forces, drive far in the direction of Vyazma, and cooperate with the Fourth Army, approaching the city from the southwest, in annihilating the encircled enemy. I was asked to report how Panzer Group 3 might be used alongside the Ninth Army. Subordinate to the panzer group were the 7th Panzer Division, the 14th Motorised Infantry Division, and the 900th Motorised Training Brigade. It would also have assigned to it (with the headquarters of the XLI and LVI Panzer

Corps) the 1st, 6th, and 8th Panzer Divisions, as well as the 36th Motorised Infantry Division.

At the headquarters of Panzer Group 3 there was unanimity that the enemy ought not to be thrown back but rather prevented from retreating behind the Dnieper and behind the Moscow defensive line. Only in this way could he be eliminated. Since an almost continuous enemy front had been formed, it would have to be penetrated before an envelopment could be carried out. Regarding the breakthrough point, we discussed three options.

The first option was to strike as far as possible to the north. The further north this took place, more enemy forces would be captured. An attack from Lake Ilmen would best fit this approach. There was still movement in this vicinity (see page 139), and no fixed front had yet been formed. Militating against such an attack at present was the inability of motorised troops to move quickly amidst the poor terrain east of the Lovat and in the Valdai Hills. Moreover, this attack would have had no cover on the northern flank, and the role of the Ninth Army would have been insignificant until it was too late. This option was discarded.

The second option was to utilise the Andreapol bridgehead for an attack over the Western Dvina from the vicinity east of Toropets, to drive eastwards on the negotiable high ground north of the Nelidovo-Olenino railway track, and then to veer south towards Vyazma. The enemy forces on the Andreapol-Bayevo sector of the Western Dvina front would thus need to be factored into the encirclement. The future supply to the panzer group would be facilitated through an assault by the bulk of the Ninth Army and through the possible exploitation of the railway between Velikiye Luki and Zapadnaya Dvina. However, for this option it was worth taking into account the imperviousness of the enemy flank, the speed of execution, and the time of year. The enemy would only be endangered once Panzer Group 3 crossed the Bely-Sychyovka line to the southeast. Yet by then enemy divisions would have had time to retreat from the front to behind the Dnieper. We could expect to become bogged down due to bad weather during the 200-kilometre drive from Andreapol to Vyazma. In addition, the short timeframe demanded rapid action along a shorter route and the abandonment of a large envelopment.

The third option, which fulfilled these conditions, was a breakthrough in the Novoselki area through Kholm towards Vyazma. With close coordination of our armoured units and with reasonably dry weather we could hope to reach the Dnieper at Kholm on the second day of the attack and to proceed towards Vyazma before the enemy could gather stronger forces. If the infantry divisions followed quickly, the anticipated encirclement front between Vyazma and Kholm (60 kilometres) could be adequately held. The disadvantage of such a restricted operation was that although the strong enemy forces southwest of Bely would come under attack, they would probably not be encircled. They would sooner or later appear on the northern flank of the Ninth Army. A further disadvantage was that, within such a narrow area, enemy horse-drawn columns would likely disrupt the movements of the rear parts of the panzer corps. It was therefore necessary to reassign neighbouring infantry divisions to Panzer Group 3.

I decided against the legitimate concerns of my advisers to recommend to Bock that the panzer group break through the front east of Novoselki in the direction of Kholm.

The headquarters of the Ninth Army had also submitted an attack plan to Army Group Centre. It intended for the V Corps to lead the main attack directly over the Vop. A panzer corps on either side was to ensure the rapid advance of the infantry. This would have ruled out an operational attack by the panzer group into the rear of the enemy position. The army group therefore ordered a breakthrough by Panzer Group 3 alone in the direction of Kholm-Vyazma. The neighbouring corps (the V and VI) were placed under the command of the panzer group.

THE THIRD ENCIRCLEMENT

The previous battles of encirclement in which Panzer Group 3 had been involved had arisen from the course of operations. These encirclements had to be improvised. Now it was a matter of breaking through the enemy front in order to provide space for a strike against him from the rear. Thorough preparation for the breakthrough was a necessary precondition for the success of the encirclement. The condition of the roads and terrain east of Novoselki allowed only one panzer corps to conduct the main thrust eastwards along a narrow strip of land. Because of the sharp bend in the front, the other panzer corps would have to begin with an off-centre advance towards Bely.

The headquarters of the LVI Panzer Corps was the first to arrive, so it was entrusted with making preparations for the drive on Kholm. For this purpose the corps was assigned the 7th and 8th Panzer Divisions, as well as the 129th Infantry Division, which was already at the front. Since the 8th Panzer Division was withheld by Army Group North at the last minute, it had to be replaced with the 6th Panzer Division. Unfortunately, this entailed the split of the XLI Panzer Corps, a unit that had existed since the beginning of the campaign. The panzer regiments of both panzer divisions were not up to full combat strength, but as the success of the breakthrough depended on a powerful armoured thrust, both regiments were to be unified under the command of the 6th Panzer Division until they reached the Dnieper. Such a measure should not ordinarily be taken in warfare, but in this case the poor road conditions justified the deprivation of the 7th Panzer Division of its strongest means of attack. Indeed, the quick thrust of the 6th Panzer Division later proved of value when a Russian tank brigade struck the southern flank of the German formation shortly before it reached the Dnieper. The 129th Infantry Division was to follow both panzer divisions so that it could be deployed along the line of encirclement east of the Dnieper.

Taking advantage of the armoured thrust to conduct its own attack, the V Corps was to cover the right flank of the LVI Panzer Corps, assist in maintaining the momentum of the breakthrough, and relieve the panzer corps east of the Dnieper as soon as possible.

A particularly difficult task fell to the XLI Panzer Corps which, aside from the 1st Panzer Division and 36th Motorised Infantry Division, had under its command the 6th Infantry Division, already committed at the front. The corps would take possession of the road junction at Bely, then the mobile divisions would turn east, cross the Dnieper north of Kholm, and secure the northern flank of Panzer Group 3 against Sychyovka. Only skillful leadership of the corps would ensure success in turning eastwards and cohesion within the panzer group.

Following the XLI Panzer Corps, the VI Corps was to attack on either side of Lomonosovo, hurl enemy forces located west of Bely into the marshland, and afterwards secure the area east of Bely against Rzhev.

Instead of discussing the tactical details of the breakthrough, I shall assess its operational results. The breakthrough succeeded surprisingly quickly in dry weather on 2 October. Once again, excellent support was provided by the VIII Air Corps. Enemy resistance at the point of penetration by German armour was lower than expected. The tanks of the LVI Panzer Corps soon punched through the woodland on the Vop, halfway between Novoselki and Kholm. Southwest of Kholm a Red tank brigade fought fiercely to the death and thereby delayed the crossing of the Dnieper. But on 4 October the 6th and 7th Panzer Divisions encountered undamaged bridges over the river, broke enemy resistance, and drove towards Vyazma. On 6 October the 7th Panzer Division stood for the third time on the highway with a reversed front, cutting off enemy forces that had too late commenced their retreat over the Dnieper. On 7 October, as the 10th Panzer Division (under Panzer Group 4) made contact with the southern wing of the 7th Panzer Division near Vyazma, the LVI Panzer Corps had created a solid line of encirclement from the city to the east of Kholm. Russian forces that had fallen back to the east conducted several violent night raids in a vain attempt to puncture this line.

Southwest of Bely, the XLI Panzer Corps had to overcome strong enemy resistance. On 4 October the corps found an opportunity to bypass Bely to the south and strike far to the east, so it left the capture of the town to the VI Corps. The panzer corps, seeking to coordinate its efforts with those of the LVI Panzer Corps, fought its way to and crossed the Dnieper on 7 October in order to cover the rear of the encirclement.

Quickly and according to plan, the V Corps passed through and to the south of Kholm and relieved the panzer divisions along the line of encirclement. Few enemy forces escaped to the east this time.

Events unfolded differently for the XXIII Corps on the upper Western Dvina. Russian forces evacuated their positions on 7 October. Many minefields caused the corps to lose contact with the enemy, who fled behind the Volga northwest of Rzhev almost without any losses.

In retrospect, the LVI Panzer Corps would have been capable of performing the breakthrough and encirclement by itself, meaning that the XLI Panzer Corps could have been more usefully employed in joint action with the XXIII Corps. Yet could the LVI Panzer Corps have carried out its envelopment manoeuvre through Kholm towards Vyazma with such certainty had it not been aware of the XLI Panzer Corps on its flank?

The encirclement was a great success. In conjunction with Panzer Groups 3 and 4, respectively, the attack by the Ninth and Fourth Armies further reduced Russian military strength by 45 large formations. By 20 October another 15 units near Bryansk perished at the hands of Panzer Group 2 and of the Second Army. The defensive front before Moscow was breached. Army Group Centre, wielding the lion's share of the German armoured forces, had gained operational freedom in the direction of the enemy capital which had been abandoned in great haste by the entire governmental apparatus (aside from Stalin himself) and by hundreds of thousands of people. The strategic objective of the campaign, Moscow, now finally lay within reach. It was hoped that its capture would permanently damage Russian political, economic, and military power. Was it now sensible to halt shortly before the objective, failing to exploit a promising situation that would probably never recur?

But on 7 October, the day on which the Vyazma pocket closed, snow began to fall across the entire Eastern Front, indicating that it was time to cease operations. The German leadership decided otherwise, ordering the capture or encirclement of Moscow by the end of the year. Panzer Group 3 took Kalinin on 14 October, Panzer Group 4 threw back the Siberian 32nd Rifle Division (which had arrived from Vladivostok) from the Moscow defensive line at Borodino on 18 October, and Panzer Group 2 proceeded partially beyond Orel on its way to Tula on 24 October. Then, however, an ally of the enemy materialised and achieved what the Russian leadership could not despite heavy casualties. Not the Russian winter but rather the autumn rain brought the German advance to a standstill. Day and night it rained and snowed incessantly. All movements bogged down in knee-deep mud. The lack of ammunition, fuel, and rations shaped the tactical and operational situation in the next few weeks.

Here we will end the description of operations. The renewal and failure of the attack on Moscow has been discussed critically and in detail elsewhere.[125] Nonetheless, it is worth commenting on a question that arises in conclusion. After the completion of the Battles of Bryansk and Vyazma in mid-October, was the German leadership justified in resuming operations with a view to encircling Moscow?

We must answer this question in the negative. After the experiences of the last few weeks, further deterioration of the roads could be expected for the rest of the year. Mobile operations, necessary to prevent the recovery of the enemy from his severe setback, would no longer be possible until winter. Yet a winter campaign would be challenging. Warm clothes, blankets, antifreeze, and stoves, though prepared, had not been delivered to the troops. Moreover, the supply situation would become more difficult the further we moved away from the railway terminals, necessitating reliance on land routes.

But even disregarding the difficulties of the weather at this time of year, the military position was less favourable than it had seemed. Panzer Group 2 was at the end of its tether as a result of its participation in the sweeping Battle of Kiev and lack of opportunity thereafter for maintenance.[126] It was doubtful whether it would reach Tula, its next objective. Even had the panzer group managed to advance as far as Gorky (400 kilometres east of Moscow), it would have been without flank protection. Panzer Groups 3 and 4, which were supposed to encircle Moscow from the north, would first have to overcome the Moskva-Volga Canal and the Volga Reservoir southeast of Kalinin. Near Mozhaysk, Panzer Group 4 encountered the first reinforcements from the Far East. Due to a shortage of fuel, Panzer Group 3 was immobilised and widely dispersed between Vyazma and Kalinin. It also suffered from a shortage of ammunition while engaged in heavy fighting in Kalinin. Along the elongated flank of the panzer group, undefeated enemy forces gathered behind the Volga northwest of Rzhev. Thus, the chances of encircling Moscow from north and south were negligible.

Clausewitz rightfully ridicules the all-knowing critics who judge a commander according to success or failure and who would have condemned Napoleon had he decided against exploiting his victory at Borodino in early September 1812. They would have exclaimed: 'Because of his timidity he failed to take the enemy capital, the defenceless Moscow, and thereby left a nucleus around which new resistance could gather.'[127] Would this condemnation be applicable to the German leadership in 1941 had it chosen to discontinue the attack against Moscow? Certainly not. Though confronting the same decision as Napoleon had, the German leadership did so not at the beginning of September but rather six weeks later. Also, this was not about the short-term pursuit of a defeated army wanting to avoid another decisive battle. Rather, it would be the final struggle with an opponent determined to defend the historic capital of the country by any means. We should have the courage to recognise that we could not remove the latent northern threat to the thrust on Moscow, that the shift of our main effort to the south in September had caused a loss of time of at least one month, and that our forces were insufficient for a double envelopment of the capital. It should also be admitted that Hitler's intention of subjugating Russia within one year could not be realised. This is unsurprising. Had we paused before the onset of winter at the watersheds of the Volga, Don, Dnieper, and Western Dvina, it could very well be interpreted as a wise act of self-restraint. Our defeat at the gates of Moscow cannot be seen as such. Rather, it restored the self-confidence of the Red Army, kindled powerful Russian national sentiment, and strengthened immensely the faith in Stalin's dictatorship. None of this was conducive to making the enemy ready to sue for peace. But these points fall into the politico-strategic area, the study of which lies beyond the scope of this book.

CONCLUSION

The historian who seeks to understand why the campaign against Russia in 1941 failed to achieve its objective despite overwhelming military victories will, among other things, arrive at three conclusions. First, the strength of Russian political and military resistance was underestimated. Second, Hitler's politico-strategic objective differed from the operational goal of the army leadership. Third, Hitler consequently intervened in the conduct of operations, eventually destroying the much-needed bond of trust between the military and political leadership. The historian will ultimately come to the conclusion that given the existing state of war it was a political mistake to attack Russia and that all military efforts were therefore doomed to failure from the outset. But despite such a negative assessment of the strategic prospects of success it was incumbent on the soldiers, insofar as it was possible, to separate operations from the general conduct of the war and to determine the expedience of such operations. Since we cannot comprehensively cover the reasons for all decisions taken during the campaign, we will not presume to be able to establish any final truth from an examination of the operations or even to develop new theories. Only with considerable reservation do we dare to compile some theories and principles for the operational use of armoured formations in an offensive. It should be noted that the following discussion relates to the conditions in 1941.

Also to be borne in mind is that the enemy air force occasionally harassed, though never effectively prevented, our operations. On the other hand, the technical equipment for the mobile formations did not meet the requirements of warfare on the Eastern Front.

1. Armoured and motorised divisions are the means by which land forces conduct operations. They are the strongest offensive weapons, but they also wear out quickly and must therefore be employed en masse.

2. The operational unit is the panzer army consisting of several panzer corps and possibly also of horse-drawn formations. The diversion of individual corps or divisions is a mistake which only leads to disappointment. The cooperation of multiple panzer armies in a joint task guarantees the greatest success.

3. Panzer armies are to be committed to an attack where the decisive battle is sought, not on secondary fronts for secondary objectives. Their distribution on a broad front with various tasks leads to their fragmentation.

4. Underlying the operations in the West in 1940 was one primary operational idea: breaking through the enemy centre, advancing to the coast, and separating the Allied armies into two parts so that they could be destroyed piecemeal. Almost all of the mobile formations interacted successfully on the decisive front (Dunkirk). In the Russian campaign there was no consistent operational plan for the whole army. The deployment orders for Barbarossa contained only tactical instructions for partial operations. The German armoured formations were scattered across the entire front. About one-third of them were absent from the final decisive battle for Moscow.

5. Armoured units are to be exploited for bold operations. Rather than trying to drive the enemy back with a frontal assault, they should seek battle with a reversed front and cut enemy

lines of communication. Inevitable crises must be taken into account when relying upon the mobility of armour.

6. Outflanking the enemy is decisive. It leads to his encirclement and destruction. The greater the number of units employed, the further the lunge of the envelopment manoeuvre. More enemy forces will then fall prey to annihilation. The space available and the forces utilised must be in harmony.

7. The use of armoured forces in the first wave of an attack is the best way to bring their mobility to bear, for their movements then remain unobstructed by horse-drawn columns. If armour and infantry must cooperate in penetrating the front and in carving out a zone of operations, it is advantageous to deploy the armoured forces on their own narrow combat sector. If armour is withheld, it subsequently has to overtake the advancing infantry, usually leading to loss of time and allowing the enemy to regroup.

8. The successes of armoured formations must be exploited fully with bold and rapid action so as to maintain the initiative and to prevent the paralysis of operations. The daring of their commanders should be upheld, not stifled. It infringes upon the inner nature of the tank arm to inhibit armoured units in their mobility (their means of protection) and to tie them down to one spot for an extended period.

9. As always in war, a surprise attack facilitates and increases the chances of success. In modern warfare this applies to armoured units. A surprise attack consists primarily in rapid movements that knock all defensive measures on the head, thereby debilitating the enemy troops and leadership. It may also involve the use of difficult terrain. Yet there are limits. Successful surprise attacks should not be allowed to degenerate into reckless actions if further surprise attacks are impossible.

10. The advance of motorised troops may be delayed due to the unforeseeable conditions of roads and bridges. Marching

orders for larger formations must allow for this by giving the troops enough time to reach their objectives.

11. The advance on a broad front, taking advantage of all serviceable routes, eases the movements of the individual elements of a formation and limits the effect of enemy air strikes. But precautions must be taken (e.g. by adopting an echelon formation in depth) to ensure that certain elements are not rendered inoperable in the clash with the enemy. Merging all of the elements on the battlefield is generally easier to bring about from in-depth rather than lateral displacements.

12. The woefully underdeveloped road network in the zone of operations of Panzer Group 3 greatly hindered movements, especially since the condition of these roads could not be ascertained from our maps. Our experiences in the Polish campaign were dwarfed by those in Russia. The excellent road network in the West had blurred the memory of conditions in the East. Most of the eastern roads were sandy in dry weather and boggy in rain. Preparations prior to the campaign failed to address the question of how to avoid traffic jams. Special measures were essential, e.g. appointing senior officers (generals) as traffic control officers, arranging troops into march groups that could be recalled, assembling labour battalions with tractors at particularly difficult spots, temporarily blocking oncoming traffic, and momentarily stopping all movements.[128]

Similarly, difficulties arose in pushing through vast woodland. Even with only low enemy resistance, positioning the troops for battle was usually impossible. As in the West (Ardennes), it proved worthwhile to allocate motorcycle infantry or cross-country vehicles, supported by a handful of tanks, to the vanguard.

13. It would have been impossible to assign to the armoured formations only terrain to which they were suited. Nevertheless, it is best to avoid impassable terrain like the Valdai Hills. In

order to prevent vehicles from undergoing wear and tear disproportionate to operational gains, they should only remain in rough terrain while operations are at a halt during bad weather. Generally, roads in the east dry quickly in summer. In extended muddy periods (spring and autumn) it is necessary to do without the operational movements of armoured formations.

In general it must be asserted that the hesitant, peacetime-inherited approach of using large armoured formations for independent operational tasks resulted in little progress during the Russian summer campaign in 1941. The organisation of armoured troops into panzer groups was a response to lessons from the French campaign and was a step in the right direction. Despite the decisive success of independent mobile formations in the Western campaign, in the East they were too strongly bound to the movements of non-motorised units. The mobile troops were often subordinated to the infantry armies in groups, corps, or divisions for tactical purposes and were thereby restricted in their operational freedom. There was no clear operational objective. We attempted through lateral displacements to offset failures in exploiting successes. However, it was too late and led to considerable attrition on vehicles and consumption of fuel. One panzer corps alone is too weak to carry out operational tasks, for it lacks flank and rear protection. Where it was possible, the joint action of several panzer corps decisively influenced the course of the campaign despite unfavourable roads and ground conditions.

Let it not be assumed that this experience is applicable in nuclear warfare, in which destruction can be wreaked far behind enemy lines. From the course, successes, and failures of past campaigns, future tank commanders will form their own opinions, develop their own ideas, and thereby improve their capability. They will do well to heed what Prince Eugene of Savoy impressed upon the young Crown Prince Frederick of Prussia: 'Continuously reflect upon your craft, upon your own undertakings, and upon the outstanding field commanders. Such reflection is

the sole means of acquiring the speed of deliberation needed to immediately comprehend a particular situation and to devise a specific solution
for it.'[129]

....

HERMANN HOTH'S CAREER AFTER THE BATTLE OF VYAZMA

BY LINDEN LYONS

Hermann Hoth was undoubtedly one of the most brilliant tank commanders of the Second World War, yet this is overshadowed by his strong enthusiasm for the expansionist and racist ideology of Nazism.

In October 1941, Hoth assumed command of the Seventeenth Army, positioned on the northern wing of Army Group South.[1] One of his first acts, on 17 November, was to issue an order on the conduct of German soldiers on the Eastern Front (see appendix 10). This order demonstrates his obsequiousness to Hitler and, according to Marcel Stein, 'cast[s] doubt on [his] sanity'.[2] It also reflects the national trauma of the loss of the First World War for which Jewish Bolshevism was blamed.[3] Hoth mimicked Hitler's views whilst also seeking to outdo a similar order by Field-Marshal Walther von Reichenau on 10 October. Specifically, Hoth referred to 'two profoundly incompatible views': 'a German sense of honour and race' versus 'Asiatic doctrines and primitive instincts inflamed by a small number of mostly Jewish intellectuals'. He stated that Germany's historic mission was to 'save European culture from the encroachment of Asiatic barbarism'. Such encroachment had lasted for two centuries, and the only result of the current conflict would be 'the annihilation of one side or the other'. There was to be no compassion towards the Russian population, which harboured 'Jewish-Bolshevik agitators', and the land was to be exploited to the benefit of the German Army and homeland.

The result of such exploitation was the starvation of the population, which thereby fueled anti-German sentiment.[4] By February 1942, Hoth was concerned about the potential for rebellion, especially in those areas which were in danger of being retaken by Russian forces. He therefore ordered the supply of food to such areas out of military necessity.[5] Nonetheless, the Seventeenth Army was still pushed back by the Russian offensive of early 1942.

At the end of May 1942, Hoth became commander of the Fourth Panzer Army. This unit was the spearhead for the summer offensive in southern Russia, commencing its advance towards the Volga on 28 June 1942.[6] By 5 July, the Fourth Panzer Army reached the Don and partook in the Battle of Voronezh. Hoth captured the western part of the city on 6 July, but had to await the arrival of the Sixth Army a few days later before he could proceed southeast towards Stalingrad.[7] However, Hitler diverted the Fourth Panzer Army southwards so as to help the First Panzer Army over the lower Don, thereby preventing Hoth from reaching Stalingrad in July.[8] By the time the Fourth Panzer Army retraced its steps, it had expended much of its fuel.[9] Furthermore, Russian forces had gathered to slow both the Fourth Panzer Army and the Sixth Army in their push on Stalingrad.[10]

Hoth crossed the Don and reached Kotelnikovo on 2 August. He approached Stalingrad from the south whilst the Sixth Army advanced from the north. Against heavy Russian resistance, the two armies rendezvoused to the west of Stalingrad on 3 September, and German troops entered the city on 13 September.[11] Yet a Russian counteroffensive in November encircled the Sixth Army, two Romanian armies, and parts of the Fourth Panzer Army in Stalingrad.[12] In December, the rest of the panzer army, now reinforced, sought to open a corridor to the city, but its advance stalled. Moreover, the commander of the Sixth Army, Colonel-General Friedrich Paulus, complied with Hitler's order to hold on to Stalingrad. The result was that the Sixth Army failed to break out (and was eventually destroyed) whilst the Fourth Panzer Army was compelled to retreat by Christmas Eve (see appendix 11). By the beginning of 1943, Hoth had withdrawn further to Rostov-on-Don, maintaining this position until early February.[13]

During this time, the Fourth Panzer Army and the First Panzer Army executed Field-Marshal Erich von Manstein's castling manoeuvre, which involved moving from the extreme right wing to the extreme left wing of the German position in the south. This manoeuvre would cover the German retreat and prepare for a counteroffensive.[14] Indeed, Russian forces overextended themselves, permitting Hoth to retake Kharkov in March 1943. On 1 March, he had already reported to Manstein that the 'attack had gone amazingly well'.[15]

Afterwards, the Fourth Panzer Army was poised on the southern edge of a salient that had formed around Kursk, while Colonel-General Walter Model's Ninth Army was ready to strike from the north.[16] Extensive planning and a considerable military build-up meant that the attack did not commence until July 1943, and in the end the Battle of Kursk was an utter failure for the German side.[17] Hoth had predicted that 'breaking through the Russian defensive system would be difficult, costly, and time-consuming', and it did indeed turn out to be the case that Russian defences were more than a match for the German forces that had been assembled.[18] Despite the slow progress of the advance, Hoth had favoured its continuation on the grounds that the destruction of the enemy's reserves had to be a precondition for the seizure of territory.[19] Yet even though he won a tactical victory with his spearhead, the II SS Panzer Corps, over the Russian 5th Guards Tank Army at Prokhorovka on 12 July, neither he nor Model achieved a breakthrough.[20] In August, Hoth was forced to retreat to the southwest in the face of a powerful Russian offensive, and by the end of September the Fourth

Panzer Army had withdrawn further west, establishing itself behind the Dnieper to the south of Kiev.[21] In conducting this retreat, Hoth understood the importance of maintaining discipline and of keeping his units intact. A disorderly withdrawal could have resulted in disaster for German forces in southern Russia. On 18 September, Hoth had stated to his corps commanders: 'The withdrawal of the army is one of the most difficult tasks it can be given. It must be mastered. If this doesn't happen, the consequences are unthinkable. It must succeed'. He concluded: 'The panzer army has resolved to get its formations back over the Dnieper, without losing a man or a weapon'.[22]

Hoth succeeded in this endeavour. Yet by November 1943, there was no way in which his depleted panzer army could hold on to Kiev against opposing Russian forces. They were not only quantitatively superior but also increasingly operationally adept, for this time they advanced without overextending.[23] Despite Hoth's excellent leadership of the Fourth Panzer Army during the previous eighteen months (not to mention the operational effectiveness with which he led Panzer Group 3 in 1941), and also despite Hoth's receipt of the Swords to the Oak Leaves to the Knight's Cross of the Iron Cross on 15 September, Hitler blamed him for the loss of Kiev and relieved him of command.[24] Only in April 1945 was he recalled to active duty in order to organise the defence of the Harz Mountains.[25] He surrendered to the Americans when the war ended in May 1945.[26]

Along with thirteen other German military leaders, Hoth was put on trial in the High Command Trial from December 1947 until October 1948. The prosecution demonstrated that orders like Hoth's of November 1941 exceeded what was required in terms of conducting Hitler's war against Russia. Such orders indicated the commitment of the army to the ideology of the regime and encouraged crimes against Russian civilians.[27] The prosecution also highlighted the eagerness of the German generals for war. Hoth had recorded his thoughts on a meeting between Hitler and his military leaders on 23 November 1939.[28] These notes reveal Hoth's agreement with Hitler's thinking:

Is there any need at all for an attack [against Luxembourg, Belgium, and Holland in 1940?] There is a general conviction that great changes in history can be brought about only by the sword. . . . Why not peace? Law of nature. Self-preservation. . . . The Führer is resolved to make a lordly decision—to fight. . . . Never before was the situation as favourable as it is now. It would be a crime not to exploit it.[29]

While the case of the prosecution was documentary, that of the defence was rhetoric.[30] In particular, the generals' defence rested on the idea that orders could not be taken as evidence of criminality, for they were issued hastily during mobile warfare.[31] Yet this position was hard to maintain for Hoth's order of 17 November 1941, a non-compulsory order wherein Hoth had carefully laid out what he saw as the historical and racial justification for the German war against Russia. There can be no doubt that he had encouraged the elimination of communists and Jews, so in the post-war trials he had to find a way to explain the vehement language he had employed.[32]

First, he claimed that this order was not widely distributed, and that he had sought merely to encourage vigilance against partisans in the Ukraine: 'The German soldier, in his good nature . . . easily forgot that he was still in the enemy's territory'. He stated that he had wanted to remind his troops of the necessity to 'break the power of Bolshevism', especially given 'the bestial cruelty of the Red Army soldiers against our prisoners and atrocities . . . committed by individual civilians'.[33]

Second, Hoth stated that he was neither anti-Semitic nor 'a friend to the Jews', and that his order was simply an accurate representation of 'the mood of the Russian Jew'. In the 1920s, Jewish 'influence in Germany's economy, in German literature, in the German press, in the theatre, in certain professions [had] brought about a strong tension in Germany'. This had wrongly resulted in Nazi 'coercive measures' against Jews, and so the hostility of Russian Jews was a reality that the German Army had to confront in 1941. Hoth then falsely asserted that he had intended no physical harm with his order and that his troops had fought 'with clean hands'.[34] He claimed that he had been unaware of the extermination of the Jews, and that he had thought that the reason for the killing of so many Jews was that it was often they who engaged in partisan warfare: 'it was a matter of common knowledge in Russia that it was the Jews in particular who participated to a very large extent in sabotage, espionage, etc.'[35]

Hoth had to defend himself against passing on the Commissar Order, which required the summary execution of the commissars of the Red Army. He argued that he had been compelled to transmit it to his troops; otherwise he would have been replaced by someone who would have done so under Hitler's close observation. He claimed that he had been opposed to the Commissar Order, despite his view that the commissar was a 'bloodthirsty beast'. He denied demanding from his soldiers the 'strictest observance' of the order. In a somewhat contradictory manner, he concluded: 'Even today I think that [Hitler's] intention really was to protect the troops against the commissars. I do not think that Hitler had any criminal intent'.[36]

In addressing the allegation of reprisals against hostages, Hoth stated that only partisans whose guilt was confirmed were executed. He further claimed that partisan warfare, 'this pest of decent warfare', resulted not from German cruelty but from Stalin's order to wage war mercilessly.[37] Additionally, Hoth had to deal with the question of the mistreatment of Russian prisoners. He said that, on the contrary, Russian prisoners were treated humanely and were never addressed in a derogatory manner (unlike the use of the term 'Boche' for German prisoners). Germans, Hoth stated, only used the friendly nickname 'Ivan', demonstrating 'the family-like relationship that our soldiers had to the Russian prisoners of war'.[38] Finally, Hoth's attorney submitted no less than ninety-two affidavits testifying to his good character.[39] Even so, he was judged guilty of war crimes and of crimes against humanity, and was sentenced to fifteen years in Landsberg Prison, where Hitler had been imprisoned in 1924.[40]

Hoth carried out his prison duties, although even after his early release in 1954 he remained convinced of his innocence.[41] He spent the rest of his life in Goslar, walking in the Harz Mountains nearby and occasionally writing about German military operations in the Second World War.[42] In addition to writing *Panzer Operations*, he wrote several articles for *Wehrkunde*.[43] From the beginning of the 1960s, he opposed the shift in the writing of military history from that by former officers to that by young German historians.[44] These historians utilised primary sources and highlighted the criminality of German warfare. In particular, he believed that they identified the campaign against Russia as the most ruthless war of conquest, enslavement, and annihilation in history.[45] Hoth thought that former officers had a greater right to craft the representation of the war. He wanted military history to focus less on German defeats and more on protecting the heroic image of the German armed forces.[46] He wished to portray a positive picture of the German art of command, especially for the benefit of subsequent generations:

> The young German faced with the decision of joining the armed forces and of becoming an officer cadet is not always deterred on material grounds. Rather, what discourages him is that there is always the feeling that you are entering a profession which no longer enjoys the respect of the general public in a way that it had in the past.[47]

To prevent this, Hoth thought that former officers should continue to write and publish. He also corresponded or spoke with journalists, military historians, and former officers in order to preserve the reputation of the army and, in particular, to defend the conduct of his former commander, Erich von Manstein, during the Stalingrad debacle.[48]

Hermann Hoth died in Goslar in 1971.

NOTES TO EPILOGUE

1 Johannes Hürter, *Hitlers Heerführer: Die deutschen Oberbefehlshaber im Krieg gegen die Sowjetunion 1941/42*, Munich: Oldenbourg, 2007, p. 635.

2 Marcel Stein, *Field Marshal von Manstein, A Portrait: The Janus Head*, Solihull, England: Helion, 2007, p. 309.

3 Benoît Lemay, *Erich von Manstein: Hitler's Master Strategist*, trans. Pierce Heyward, Havertown, PA: Casemate, 2010, p. 262.

4 Manfred Oldenburg, *Ideologie und militärisches Kalkül: Die Besatzungspolitik der Wehrmacht in der Sowjetunion 1942*, Cologne: Böhlau Verlag, 2004, p. 309.

5 *Ibid.*, pp. 311–2.

6 Antony Beevor, *Stalingrad*, London: Penguin, 1999, p. 75.

7 J.F.C. Fuller, *A Military History of the World, Vol. III: From the Seven Days Battle, 1862, to the Battle of Leyte Gulf, 1944*, New York: Funk & Wagnalls, 1954, p. 522.

8 Glantz, *When Titans Clashed: How the Red Army Stopped Hitler*, Lawrence, KS: University Press of Kansas, 1995, p. 119; Basil H. Liddell Hart, *The German Generals Talk*, New York: Morrow, 1948, pp. 204–5.

9 Joel Hayward, *Stopped at Stalingrad: The Luftwaffe and Hitler's Defeat in the East, 1942–1943*, Lawrence, KS: University Press of Kansas, 1998, p. 156.

10 Liddell Hart, *The German Generals Talk*, pp. 204–5.

11 Peter Antill, *Stalingrad 1942*, Oxford: Osprey, 2007, pp. 44–51, 55.

12 *Ibid.*, pp. 73–5; Mungo Melvin, *Manstein: Hitler's Greatest General*, London: Weidenfeld & Nicolson, 2010, p. 285; Lemay, *Erich von Manstein*, p. 301.

13 Melvin, *Manstein*, pp. 311, 327; Lemay, *Erich von Manstein*, pp. 301–2, 308, 318.

14 Melvin, *Manstein*, p. 330; Lemay, *Erich von Manstein*, p. 349; Robert M. Citino, *The Wehrmacht Retreats: Fighting a Lost War, 1943*, Lawrence, KS: University Press of Kansas, 2012, p. 66.

15 Hermann Hoth, report to Erich von Manstein, 1 March 1943, cited in Melvin, *Manstein*, p. 342.

16 Citino, *The Wehrmacht Retreats*, pp. 130–1.

17 *Ibid.*, pp. 133–6.

18 Hermann Hoth, report to Erich von Manstein, c. July 1943, cited in Melvin, *Manstein*, p. 368.

19 Melvin, *Manstein*, pp. 375–6, 380.

20 Citino, *The Wehrmacht Retreats*, p. 202; Lemay, *Erich von Manstein*, pp. 373–4.

21 Citino, *The Wehrmacht Retreats*, pp. 229–30; Melvin, *Manstein*, p. 397.

22 Hermann Hoth, statement to his corps commanders, 18 September 1943, cited in Melvin, *Manstein*, p. 397.

23 Melvin, *Manstein*, pp. 401–3.

24 *Ibid.*, pp. 212, 404; Franz Kurowski, *Panzer Aces III: German Tank Commanders in Combat in World War II*, trans. David Johnston, Mechanicsburg, PA: Stackpole, 2010, p. 153.

25 Kurowski, *Panzer Aces III*, p. 153; Charles Winchester, *Hitler's War on Russia*, Oxford: Osprey, 2007, p. 170.

26 Samuel W. Mitcham, *Triumphant Fox: Erwin Rommel and the Rise of the Afrika Korps*, Mechanicsburg, PA: Stackpole, 2009.

27 Valerie Geneviève Hébert, *Hitler's Generals on Trial: The Last War Crimes Tribunal at Nuremberg*, Lawrence, KS: University Press of Kansas, 2010, p. 94.

28 *Ibid.*, pp. 76–7.

29 Hermann Hoth, notes, 23 November 1939, cited in Hébert, *Hitler's Generals on Trial*, p. 77.

30 Hébert, *Hitler's Generals on Trial*, p. 114.

31 *Ibid.*, p. 108.

32 Lemay, *Erich von Manstein*, p. 259.

33 Hermann Hoth, testimony, 1948, cited in Hébert, *Hitler's Generals on Trial*, p. 121.

34 *Ibid.*

35 *Ibid.*, p. 122.

36 *Ibid.*, p. 116. It is noteworthy that there is little evidence of implementation of the Commissar Order by the Seventeenth Army in late 1941 and early 1942, i.e. whilst Hoth commanded this formation. This indicates neither opposition to the Commissar Order nor compassion towards political commissars. Rather, the realities of the battlefield and the security of German troops took priority over ideological pursuits (Robert B. Bernheim, *The Commissar Order and the Seventeenth German Army: From Genesis to Implementation, 30 March 1941–31 January 1942*, PhD thesis, Montreal: McGill University, 2004, p. 461).

37 Hermann Hoth, testimony, 1948, cited in Hébert, *Hitler's Generals on Trial*, p. 117.

38 *Ibid.*, p. 123.

39 Hébert, *Hitler's Generals on Trial*, pp. 113–4.

40 *Ibid.*, p. 151; Samuel W. Mitcham, *Blitzkrieg No Longer: The German Wehrmacht in Battle, 1943*, Barnsley, South Yorkshire: Pen & Sword, 2010, p. 295.

41 Hébert, *Hitler's Generals on Trial*, pp. 192–3.

42 *Ibid.*, pp. 193–4.

43 Articles by Hermann Hoth include: 'Buchbesprechung zu Jacobsen, "Fall Gelb",' *Wehrkunde*, vol. 7 (1958), no. 2, pp. 118–9; 'Mansteins Operationsplan

für den Westfeldzug 1940 und die Aufmarschanweisung des O.K.H. vom 27. Februar 1940', *Wehrkunde*, vol. 7 (1958), no. 3, pp. 127–30; 'Das Schicksal der französischen Panzerwaffe im 1. Teil des Westfeldzugs 1940', *Wehrkunde*, vol. 7 (1958), no. 7, pp. 367–77; 'Zu "Mansteins Operationsplan für den Westfeldzug 1940 und die Aufmarschanweisung des O.K.H. vom 27. 2. 40"', *Wehrkunde*, vol. 7 (1958), no. 8, p. 459; 'Der Kampf von Panzerdivisionen in Kampfgruppen in Beispielen der Kriegsgeschichte', *Wehrkunde*, vol. 8 (1959), no. 11, pp. 576–84; and 'Die Verwendung von Panzern in der Verteidigung und die Neugliederung der deutschen NATO-Divisionen 1959', *Wehrkunde*, vol. 8 (1959), no. 12.

44 Oliver von Wrochem, *Erich von Manstein: Vernichtungskrieg und Geschichtspolitik*, 2nd edition, Paderborn: Ferdinand Schöningh, 2009, p. 287.

45 *Ibid.*, pp. 288–9, including n. 29. Examples of such historians and their works: Hans-Adolf Jacobsen, *Fall Gelb: Der Kampf um den deutschen Operationsplan zur Westoffensive*, Wiesbaden, 1957; Martin Broszat, *Nationalsozialistische Polenpolitik 1939–1945*, Stuttgart, 1961; Ernst Nolte, *Der Faschismus in seiner Epoche: Die action francaise, der italienische Faschismus, der Nationalsozialismus*, Munich, 1963; Helmut Krausnick, 'Hitler und die Morde in Polen', *Vierteljahreshefte für Zeitgeschichte*, vol. 11 (1963), pp. 196–210; Andreas Hillgruber, *Hitlers Strategie: Politik und Kriegsführung 1940–1941*, Munich, 1965.

46 Wrochem, *Erich von Manstein*, p. 288.

47 Hermann Hoth, c. 1960, cited in Wrochem, *Erich von Manstein*, p. 288, n. 27.

48 Wrochem, *Erich von Manstein*, p. 304. For instance, Hoth used his connection with Paul Carell (aka SS Lieutenant-Colonel Paul Karl Schmidt) in order to encourage a positive picture of Manstein's record at Stalingrad in Carell's books (p. 306).

APPENDIX 1A

....

Panzer Group 3
Operations Section No. 25/41
Top Secret / Chiefs of Staff

General Staff Headquarters
12 March 1941

Deployment orders for 'Barbarossa'

1. *Overall objective*

In the event that Russia changes its present attitude towards Germany, precautionary measures are to be taken that enable pre-emptive action against Soviet Russia and the overthrow of its armed forces in a quick campaign before such forces can retreat into the depths of Russian territory.

For the conduct of battle, the principles tried and tested in the Polish campaign will be applied. The impact of the enemy air force against the German army can be expected to be greater than in the past. The troops must be prepared for the use of chemical weapons by the enemy, even from the air. This might motivate us to favour rapid dispersal over methodical action.

However, the top priority for this campaign to be hammered home to every commander and soldier is: *Rapid and ruthless progress!* The offensive on the entire front is to be sustained through the decisive use of weapons and the tireless pursuit of the enemy. Tanks, strong artillery, and medium weaponry are to be pushed far forward for this purpose. Only in this way will it be possible to tear apart the Russian army and to annihilate most of the forces still on this side of the Dnieper-Western Dvina line.[130]

2. *Enemy position*

The current distribution of troops makes it likely that Russia is determined to fight west of the Dnieper and the Western Dvina with nothing less than the strongest of forces that will exploit both the sporadically reinforced field fortifications on the new and old frontiers as well as the several, more defensible streams and watercourses. . . .

3. *Army Group Centre* shall begin the attack on B-Day,[131] Y o'clock, between Brest-Litovsk and the Rominter Heath with the Fourth Army on the right and the Ninth Army on the left. The army group will enter Russian territory, advance (with Panzer Groups 2 and 3 ahead on the wings) on both sides of Minsk to the vicinity around and to the north of Smolensk, and annihilate the enemy forces in Belarus in order to create a position from which to continue operations further east or northeast.

The *Ninth Army* is to thrust with the bulk of its forces either side of Grodno and with the remainder alongside Panzer Group 3 in the general direction of Lida and Vilnius.

Panzer Group 2, in the sector of the Fourth Army, is to advance its left wing from Brest-Litovsk to Minsk via Baranovichi.

Army Group North will advance with the southern wing of the Sixteenth Army (the 32nd Infantry Division of the II Corps) on Kovno and with Panzer Group 4 on Dünaburg.

4. *Panzer Group 3*, to be subordinated to the high command of the Ninth Army before charging ahead on the left wing of the army group, will force its way through the enemy situated west of the Neman towards Merkine, Olita, and Prienai and will capture these crossings. Without awaiting the rear divisions, the panzer group will conduct a strike against enemy forces presumed to be near Vilnius and will separate

them from Minsk. With the aim of outflanking to the north enemy forces near Minsk, the panzer group will advance to the Molodechno-Lake Naroch line, ready to move eastwards in the direction of Borisov. The panzer group will then cooperate with Panzer Group 2, approaching from the southwest, in the annihilation of the forces near Minsk or will continue its manoeuvre of encirclement towards the upper Western Dvina in the direction of Vitebsk and further north. . . .

5. *Orders*

(a) The *LVII Panzer Corps* will cross the frontier between Lake Pomorze and Lake Galadus with the spearheads of a panzer division and a motorised infantry division, head towards the Druskieniki-Merkine sector of the Neman, force a crossing of the river at Merkine, and thereafter drive north of the Ruska Forest through Varena to the Lida-Vilnius road without awaiting the advance of the XXXIX Panzer Corps from Olita on Vilnius. So as to be able to force a way to the Berzniki-Seirijai road, an artillery-reinforced infantry regiment of the V Corps will be put under the command of the LVII Panzer Corps.

The LVII Panzer Corps is to capture and cross the 16-ton bridge at Merkine, which shall then be handed over to the V Corps. Later, while protecting the flank against Lida, the LVII Panzer Corps will occupy Oshmyany and the region to its south so that the Minsk-Vilnius link will be severed. It may be necessary for a panzer division to veer in the direction of Vilnius in support of the XXXIX Panzer Corps.

The LVII Panzer Corps shall then seize the area between Volozhin and Molodechno and stand by for an advance in the direction of Borisov. It is either to establish contact with Panzer Group 2 or, together with the XXXIX Panzer Corps, to cross the Viliya at and to the south of Smorgon so as to prevent an enemy retreat to Dokshitsy.

Depending on the development of the situation near Grodno, the main forces of the 18th Motorised Infantry Division are to follow the southern wing either through Suwalki-Augustow-Grodno or through Suwalki-Merkine.

(b) The *V Corps*, without the aforementioned infantry regiment, will break through the enemy frontier guard, move on Lazdijai, and advance towards and over the Neman at and to the south of Nemunaitis. In this connection, it is the responsibility of the corps to support the LVII Panzer Corps in its fight through the narrow Seirijai region and to clear and secure the Lazdijai-Seirijai-Olita road for the following mobile forces.

After crushing initial enemy resistance, strong advance detachments are to gain an early foothold on the east bank of the Neman, enable the crossing of further forces, and reconnoitre the east bank.

An 8-ton emergency bridge shall be constructed in good time.

After the LVII Panzer Corps has crossed the river, the 16-ton bridge at Merkine will be available to the V Corps.

(c) The *XXXIX Panzer Corps*, spearheaded by two panzer divisions, shall quickly crush enemy resistance either side of the Suwalki-Kalvarija road then advance south of Lake Zuvintas towards Olita and force the Neman crossing. The 16-ton military bridge and 16-ton bridge near Olita are to be captured. Once the armoured formations are ready on the east bank of the Neman, they are to advance on Vilnius from the south and west and push the enemy back over the Viliya. Cover against Kovno is to be effected by the rearward motorised infantry, whose subsequent advance to the north bank of the Viliya may be advantageous against Vilnius. After repelling, but not pursuing, enemy forces northwards through Vilnius, the panzer divisions will advance over the Viliya in the direction of Kobylniki. The motorised infantry divisions shall mop up Vilnius and follow behind the left wing of the corps.

Thereafter, the corps shall either attack the rear of the enemy near Minsk via Dolhinov and Dokshitsy or circle towards Polotsk via Glubokoye.

(d) The *VI Corps*, breaking through between Szeszupka and Lake

Vistytis in left echelon formation, will fight its way to Prienai, force the crossing over the Neman, and keep it open for the 14th and 20th Motorised Infantry Divisions.

The corps will cover the left flank of the advancing XXXIX Panzer Corps by rapidly acquiring the area to the north of Kalvarija and by mopping up the woods to the northeast.

As soon as the tactical situation allows, strong advance detachments are to gain an early foothold on the east bank of the Neman, enable the crossing of further forces, and reconnoitre the east bank.

In Prienai an 8-ton bridge is to be built and initially kept free for the bulk of the 14th and 20th Motorised Infantry Divisions to cross.

(e) After crossing the Neman, Panzer Group 3 will be removed from its subordination to the Ninth Army, though the latter will retain control of the V and VI Corps. For this purpose the High Command of the Ninth Army has ordered: 'In the further course of the operation the VI Corps will advance in the direction of Vilnius and the vicinity to its north. For the V Corps both the advance in the direction of Varena and Voronovo (contact with the VIII Corps) and in the direction of and to the south of Vilnius (contact with the VI Corps) may come into question'.

6.-17. etc.

APPENDIX 1B

....

Panzer Group 3
Operations Section No. 205/41
Top Secret / Chiefs of Staff
16 June 1941

GROUP ORDER FOR THE ATTACK
ACROSS THE REICH FRONTIER

1. *Enemy*
     Security detachments are on the border, with strong forces in the
  lake region between the border and the Neman. No systematic, coherent defence has thus far been detected on the Neman.
2. *Panzer Group 3* will fight its way to the Neman in the direction of
  Merkine, Olita, and Prienai, and will force a crossing over the river.
  At 3·30 a.m. on 23 June 1941, having moved into position at night,
  the panzer group shall deploy for action across the frontier
3. The *LVII Panzer Corps* will push forward with parts of the 18th Motorised Infantry Division to the south of and on the Berzniki-Kapci-
  amiestis road through Leipalingis towards Merkine. The 12th Panzer
  Division will advance on both sides of Lake Zapsys and, covering
  against Lazdijai, will laterally attack and immediately repair the Berzniki-Seirijai road. For this purpose the reinforced 109th Infantry Regiment shall be transferred from the V Corps to the LVII Panzer Corps.
     After clearing the road to Leipalingis, the panzer corps will hasten

178

towards and cross the Neman on either side of Merkine, capturing the Merkine bridge site on B-Day. The construction of a 16-ton bridge is to commence forthwith.

Parts of the Brandenburg Training Regiment are to be subordinated to the panzer corps.

4. The *V Corps*, minus a reinforced infantry regiment (see section 3), shall attack either side of Lake Dusia in the direction of Nemunaitis in order to support the advance of the LVII and XLI Panzer Corps. The V Corps will drive rapidly through Lazdijai, prevent the advance of enemy forces against the northern wing of the LVII Panzer Corps, as well as clear and mend immediately the Lazdijai-Seirijai road so that it can be used by the following motorised infantry.

After crushing initial enemy resistance, strong advance detachments are to gain an early foothold on the east bank of the Neman, enable the crossing of further forces, and reconnoitre the east bank.

A 6-ton emergency bridge shall be constructed. After the LVII Panzer Corps has crossed the river, the 16-ton bridge at Merkine will be available to the V Corps.

5. The *XXXIX Panzer Corps* shall use all available means of combat to break enemy resistance either side of the Suwalki-Kalvarija road and to the north. It will then veer to the east, cross the Sesupe, and advance on both sides of Simnas towards Olita. The panzer corps shall retain control of Kalvarija until the approach of the VI Corps. The bridge there is to be reconstructed so that it will have a capacity of 8 tons for subsequent use by two-way rear formation traffic. Parts of the 20th Motorised Infantry Division are to be sent through Mockava in order to open the way for advance of the panzer divisions towards the Sesupa. The headquarters of Panzer Group 3 shall determine whether they ought to proceed northwards through Lazdijai or Seirijai, thereby preparing an advance towards the narrow Krosna-Simnas region.

Upon reaching Olita the Neman is to be crossed at both bridge sites. Every opportunity to take the bridges intact should be fully utilised.

The bulk of the 20th Motorised Infantry Division will initially be withheld to be repositioned later. The 14th Motorised Infantry Division shall be committed only if approved by the headquarters of Panzer Group 3.

The staff and the 2nd Company of the 1st Mine-Clearance Battalion is to be put under the command of the panzer corps.

6. The *VI Corps* will fight its way to Prienai, force the crossing over the Neman, build along a part of the Prienai-Birstonas road an 8-ton bridge, and keep open the crossing for the motorised infantry divisions of the XXXIX Panzer Corps.

For this purpose the VI Corps, in left echelon formation, will attack with a strong right wing to the north of the Sesupa in order to support the advance of the XXXIX Panzer Corps. By rapidly reaching the heights to the north of Kalvarija the VI Corps will cover the left flank of the XXXIX Panzer Corps and thereafter will take the Sesupa crossings in Liudvinavas and Mariampol. The Kalvarija-Mariampol road is to be cleared and secured.

As soon as the tactical situation allows, strong advance detachments are to gain an early foothold on the east bank of the Neman, enable the crossing of further forces, and reconnoitre the east bank.

On the order of the panzer group the 8-ton bridge built near Prienai will be cleared for the bulk of the 14th and 20th Motorised Infantry Divisions to cross.

7.-13. etc.

APPENDIX 2

. . . .

Directive for the conduct of operations by Panzer Group 3

PART I: GENERAL DIRECTIONS

1. *The enemy*

   The efforts of the Russian to protect his newly annexed territories and to maintain the connection between the Baltic and Black Seas, his current concentration of troops in the western military districts, as well as his poor lines of communication make it likely that he will try at the border, at the Neman, and further east, but in any case west of the Dnieper-Western Dvina line, to bring our advance to a standstill through defence and counterattacks.

   Such an attempt would fit in with our intentions. Nevertheless, it must be expected that after some initial setbacks the enemy will retreat with delaying action from the Neman to the Dnieper and the Western Dvina, doing his best to avoid becoming embedded in bloody battles. Even as some his units flee, he will probably conduct relief attacks with strong mechanised forces against our flanks. This approach of defence and counterattack would correspond to his national character, his history, and his geopolitical position, the principal value of all of which lies in the vast space.

2. It is essential for the conduct of operations by the panzer group that the enemy is not given time to withdraw his main forces to the Dnieper-Western Dvina line. The panzer corps must reach this line

181

first by overcoming any obstacles the enemy has prepared as well as any resistance his rear guards pose. Any attack against the enemy west of the Western Dvina should not be an end in itself but must serve goal of reaching this river. The panzer group is to pierce, envelop, or bypass, but not strike, enemy forces west of the Viliya. Their annihilation is the responsibility of the following Ninth Army. The panzer group must always strive to outflank the enemy and also to drive further eastwards by night, regardless of the threat to the flank and the rear. Repeatedly throwing back enemy rear guards would be unprofitable. We must cut off the main forces of the enemy from their route of retreat to the Western Dvina. It is to be impressed on each soldier of Panzer Group 3 that the goal of every action is to: *Cross the Neman, break through to the Western Dvina.*

. . .

PART III: ORGANISATION OF TROOPS FOR
THE ADVANCE ACROSS THE BORDER

5. All measures are to be taken to ensure that the panzer divisions reach the Neman on the first day of the attack, that they start to cross the river in the evening, and that bridge construction commences at night. If the enemy is given time to throw reinforcements at the Neman overnight, then the crossing the next morning will involve greater casualties.

6. The organisation of troops and the method of attack are governed by our intelligence on the terrain and the enemy at the frontier. As the situation becomes clearer, preparations for the attack will continue to be modified accordingly. The order for the attack will only be issued shortly before the troops are assembled.

7. The preparations by the panzer divisions should consider the following:

    (a) The divisions are ready to enter the final assembly area so as to be organised for the attack. Regrouping once the advance is underway is to be avoided.

(b) In order to quickly crush initial enemy resistance and to ensure the breakthrough of the infantry towards and over the Neman, the panzer regiments are to be concentrated as far as possible beforehand and are to be protected by artillery and tank destroyers.

(c) Following the tanks will be the mobile forces (infantry on motorcycles and in armoured cars) and the pioneers. Sending medium artillery (howitzers) along with them would be advantageous.

(d) Where the terrain forbids the use of tanks (e.g. in the territory to be traversed by the LVII Panzer Corps), the divisions are to first deploy the infantry followed by medium artillery and pioneers for the removal of obstacles. If necessary, assault troops shall be detached to raid individual strongpoints and obstacles. It is important for the mobile troops to keep moving in order to quickly exploit any success.

(e) Having cleared away any obstacles, the motorised infantry with heavy weapons, the artillery, and the pioneers will use all roads to advance on the Neman in readiness to utilise fully the armoured breakthrough. Before the main forces cross the river, reconnaissance patrols of the artillery and pioneers shall go first in armoured cars or on motorcycles so as to reconnoitre the crossing points.

(f) To be kept in reserve are:
- the infantry battalions not needed for the initial advance,
- the pioneers and bridge columns assigned to the construction of bridges over the Neman,
- most of the reconnaissance battalions and tank destroyers,
- the panzer regiments for as long as the terrain prohibits their use, and
- the supply vehicles.

(g) Reflection on the destruction to be expected must inform the allocation of pioneers and bridging equipment for the removal of obstacles, the repair of roads, and the bridging of streams.

(h) A reinforced motorised infantry regiment of the 18th Motorised Infantry Division is to be incorporated into the forward part of the

12th Panzer Division as the spearhead of the LVII Panzer Corps for its drive on the Neman.

(i) Thus, advance guards will charge ahead over the border and will be followed by several spearheads of the divisions. This second wave must be positioned in readiness to go forth with the strongest fighting power (tanks and medium artillery).

8. *Vehicles*

(a) See special order for the arrangement of the combat vehicles into groups and for the assignments to be given to the vehicles at the rear.

(b) Supply convoys, logistical services, and other motor vehicles are to remain in the rear area and will follow the combat troops of the second wave.

(c) The troops must be prepared to be without *field* kitchens during the first few days of the attack.

(d) The fuel and lubricants supply columns are to be allocated to the march groups in a manner that enables immediate supply by exchanging containers. The V and VI Corps will issue corresponding orders for their subordinate units.

PART IV: PENETRATION THROUGH THE LAKE AREA WEST OF THE NEMAN

9. The objective of the penetration of the border zone by the panzer divisions is not to clear enemy forces from the west bank of the Neman but to seize, secure, and repair a road for the transportation of troops and cargo along the route of advance to the river.

In this connection the V and VI Corps will support Panzer Group 3 by attacking and destroying enemy forces in their combat sector.

10. The main roads themselves will already be occupied by the enemy and barricaded in depth. The first attack is therefore to be executed off rather than on the roads. Our troops will reach the roads to the rear of the enemy forces, prevent their retreat to the east, and com-

mence with the repair of damaged roads. After establishing a route eastwards for the German troops, those equipped with heavy weapons shall proceed further on foot while the pioneers clear the route for vehicles. In the first few days the forward units have to be prepared to carry their heavy weapons over long distances on foot. But where road conditions are good and enemy activity is low, the motorised troops must drive forwards from the rear.

11. Russian border posts, security detachments, and crossings are to be raided by small assault detachments before the enemy can sound the alarm and destroy civil engineering structures. These raids thus require astuteness, suddenness, boldness, and ruthlessness. They must also deactivate enemy bombs.

12. The motorised units assembled for the push to the Neman are only to move forward once their roads are passable. In so doing, heavy weapons and medium artillery are to be advanced far forward. Vehicles not required for combat (fuel trucks, equipment trucks, field kitchens, and signal vehicles) should be kept to the rear.

13. The second wave of the divisions, the bridge columns needed at the Neman, and the following vehicles shall move not in small jumps but directly forward from their shelter once their route of advance is free.

14. The closer the troops come to the Neman, the more they must strive, regardless of their threatened flanks, to reach and cross the river before the enemy can organise resistance. If it is possible to take intact any of the bridges over the Neman, it will be a success of vital importance.

15. As the attack begins, the corps headquarters will relieve the frontline divisions of traffic regulation in their assembly area so that divisional supervision officers can focus on keeping clear the route of advance to the Neman. An accumulation of vehicles close to the Neman is to be prevented by the timely occupation of jump-off lines across the river.

16. All vehicles shall cross the Reich frontier fueled to capacity.

....

Panzer Group 3
Operations Section
Group Command Post
3 July 1941

GROUP ORDER NO. 10 FOR 4 AND 5 JULY 1941

1. Enemy: see attached Intelligence Report No. 10.
2. On 3 July 1941 the headquarters of the Fourth Army, redesignated Fourth Panzer Army, will assume command of Panzer Groups 2 and 3.

   Panzer Group 2 shall force the crossing over the Dnieper in the Rogachev-Orsha sector and advance with most of its forces along the Minsk-Moscow highway to a line extending from the south of the Yelnya heights to the east of Yartsevo.

   The high command of the Ninth Army will take over the obstacle line extending to Rakov. The XXIII Corps is to follow the LVII Panzer Corps with the right wing of the 206th Infantry Division through Vilnius, Niemenczyn, and Podbrodzie. The 900th Motorised Training Brigade will reach Minsk on 4 July.
3. Panzer Group 3 shall break through the Vitebsk-Dzisna sector of the Western Dvina, overcome the enemy in the Smolensk-Vitebsk region in cooperation with Panzer Group 2, and reach the Beresnevo-Velizh-Nevel line.

4. Orders:

(a) Exploiting the advance of the LVII Panzer Corps, the XXXIX Panzer Corps shall attack over the Vitebsk-Ula sector of the Western Dvina and then, without stopping, drive to the Beresnevo-Velizh line, guarding the flank against the enemy in the woodlands surrounding Dobromysli. Contact is to be maintained with Panzer Group 2 (XLVII Panzer Corps).

(b) The LVII Panzer Corps shall force the Western Dvina crossing at Dzisna and advance further with the southern wing to the Velizh-Nevel line via Gorodok in order to release the XXXIX Panzer Corps for its push on Vitebsk. Reconnaissance on the northern flank for the purpose of sending the main forces of the LVII Panzer Corps to the north of the headwaters of the Western Dvina via Velikiye Luki. The remaining forces shall advance through Usvyaty and Kresty.

(c) Group Harpe (12th Panzer Division and 14th Motorised Infantry Division) shall cooperate with the Ninth Army and Panzer Group 2 in barring enemy escape routes east of Minsk. Following the arrival of all of the troops of the Ninth Army our own forces are to be relieved from the obstacle line and assembled for departure to the northeast.

. . .

11. Command posts:

Panzer Group 3	1 km south of Giedziewicze (14 km southwest of Dolhinov)
XXXIX Panzer Corps	7 km east of Dokshitsy, on the Dokshitsy-Lepel road
LVII Panzer Corps	Glubokoye

Signature

INTELLIGENCE REPORT No. 10

1. Scattered groups and combined units of the enemy in the Vitebsk-

Dzisna-Lake Naroch-Borisov region only managed to destroy a few bridges during our advance.

Russian withdrawal from Orsha to Smolensk: to protect Moscow? Little enemy activity in the (Orsha)-Vitebsk-Drissa region in the wake of our earlier success in crossing the lower Western Dvina downstream of Dünaburg indicates that the Russians, short of time and manpower, will not defend Vitebsk-Dzisna. Only local resistance at the bridgeheads or ferrying sites and the utilisation of obsolete fortifications can be expected.

Besides two unoccupied airfields around Dretun (30 kilometres northeast of Polotsk) and antiaircraft guns in Vitebsk, Polotsk, and Gorodok, no enemy forces have been observed northeast of the Western Dvina up to Surazh (45 kilometres northeast of Vitebsk) and Nevel.

2. The Bialystok pocket has been closed with over 160,000 prisoners taken. The bloody casualties of this enemy group are estimated to be several times greater, and the captured materiel appears to be vast.

The Novogrudok pocket nears disintegration. On 2 July the 12th Panzer Division alone took 30,000 prisoners.

3. Etc.

APPENDIX 4

....

My assessment of the situation on 7 July 1941 (excerpts)

Since the beginning of July the enemy succeeded, despite our expectations, in building a new defensive front behind the Western Dvina. Three or four fresh divisions and a tank division had been brought up from the interior of the Russian empire. On 4 July this line of defence was penetrated at Dzisna by the 19th Panzer Division. With heavy counterattacks by two divisions, the enemy tried in vain to wrest the bridgehead away from us. However, he managed to bring our advance on Polotsk to a standstill. The attacks by the Russian 98th and 174th Rifle Divisions against the 19th Panzer Division continue. Apparently the enemy wants to hold on to Polotsk at all costs.

. . . In its advance on Ula on the Western Dvina the 20th Panzer Division literally drowned in mud due to persistent rain. It has now extracted itself. Offensive scheduled for 3 p.m. Strong Russian forces near Ula prepared to defend. The offensive becomes difficult.

The 7th Panzer Division was to take Vitebsk like a bolt out of the blue, but already encountered resistance at Beshenkovichi, and later also in the sector north of Dombrova. Impression that there are strong forces south of Vitebsk, so the advance is suspended until the city is enveloped from the north. Meanwhile, strong enemy attacks along the entire Senno-Dombrova front. Neither concern nor freedom of action.

Employment of the 12th Panzer Division: too late on the northern wing.

. . . (one sheet missing) . . . Possibility of an encirclement of the enemy retreating eastwards to and through Smolensk by sending strong forces from the north of Vitebsk to Velizh and Usvyaty. These roads are clear of the enemy and remain undamaged. An advance on Rudnya and Demidov will be impeded by Russian rear guards, so only smaller forces will be positioned before them. The bulk of the XXXIX Panzer Corps is to veer towards Velizh (7th Panzer Division) and Usvyaty (20th Panzer and 20th Motorised Infantry Divisions). Henceforth it is crucial that the formations subordinate to the LVII Panzer Corps reach Nevel so that they can strike the rear of the Ukrainian division currently advancing from this town towards Gorodok.

(In the possession of the author)

APPENDIX 5

....

Telephone briefing by the chief of the WFSt, Colonel-General Alfred Jodl, to the commander in chief of the army, Field-Marshal Walther von Brauchitsch, on 5 July 1941

The moment approaches when the decision concerning the further conduct of operations, in particular the future use of the panzer groups, must be made. Since this decision will be crucial, perhaps the primary one for the outcome of the war, the chief of the WFSt considers it necessary that the commander in chief of the army, before defining further tasks, discusses his opinion and his objectives with the Führer. Specifically, the following questions will need to be thought through by the Führer:

1. Will Army Group North alone be strong enough to protect its eastern flank while wiping away the enemy in northwest Russia, or will a diversion of Panzer Group 3 to the northeast be necessary? After crossing the Dnieper-Western Dvina line, is the immediate veering of Panzer Group 3 to the northeast possible? In this connection, how far will flank protection to the east extend?
2. Immediately after crossing the Dnieper, is turning the Fourth Panzer Army in a southerly direction to be considered? How is the question of flank protection to be resolved?

(Documents for the Nuremberg Trials 1946–48, General Staff of the Army, Operations Section, Barbarossa)

APPENDIX 6

....

My letter to the commander of Army Group Centre,
Field-Marshal Fedor von Bock, between 22 and 26 July 1941

Field-Marshal!

Allow me to express my most humble thanks for the congratulations on the Oak Leaves. . . . It is a great honour for me to have earned it under your leadership.

Unfortunately, the standstill of the last few days so far remains unaccompanied by any significant recuperation for our forces. Our vehicles are considerably hindered by the now abysmal roads. Engine maintenance is impossible whilst we remain in constant preparedness against Russian breakthroughs and relief attempts. Nevertheless, there is an increase in the fighting capacity of those divisions that have had an opportunity to rest. My only concern is that the weakness of the 14th Motorised Infantry Division currently precludes it from performing any task.

Combat vehicle losses now amount to approximately 60 percent. If we are given ten days and sent spare parts, we would probably regain 60–70 percent of our target inventory. The total losses of other vehicles are relatively low, about seven percent, and even lower for motorcycles. Replacement officers and enlisted personnel are gradually approaching. Hopefully, the infantry divisions will provide us with the men we need. Also, about 10 days are required for the replenishment of fuel.

. . .

Signature
(Outline in the possession of the author)

APPENDIX 7

....

My assessment of the situation on 27 July 1941

The enemy position south of the highway remains unclear. Both divisions apparently encountered only weak Russian forces. It is doubtful whether the enemy still has the strength to attack from the east. Assaults from Dorogobuzh are to be expected for as long as the enemy retains mobility. The escape of some enemy troops across the Dnieper south of Ratchino cannot be prevented by the forces of the panzer group.

On and to the north of the highway extending to Bely, the enemy succeeded through the fighting of the last few days in creating a defensive front ahead of the Dnieper-Volga line of defence. Behind this front to the north of Yartsevo and partly to the west of the Vop are three or four Siberian and other divisions, to the southwest of Bely are two Siberian divisions and a mechanised division, and in the gap of the enemy forces concentrated near Toropets are two newly formed Caucasian cavalry divisions.

In the past few days Russian divisions on the Vop front attacked with little momentum and thereby suffered considerable losses. Only the strength of their heavy artillery was noteworthy. Not only has the enemy reorganised or activated new units; he is attacking repeatedly, especially near Yartsevo.

The combat strength of the Bely group can be assessed as being lower. Their cavalry divisions were hastily activated and inadequately equipped.

The long-term offensive aims and reinforcements of the enemy cannot be identified. He seems to have the intention of delaying our advance against the still unprepared Dnieper position, clearly unaware of our plan to halt the mobile formations.

The focal point for Panzer Group 3 still lies in the south in closing the pocket on the Dnieper and in covering the encirclement against attacks from the east. The extension of the southern wing beyond the highway and the persistent attempts by the enemy to attack on the Vop front place such strain on our forces that the onslaught against the road junction at Bely had to be postponed. The troops assembled for this purpose are needed to support the eastern front of the panzer group.

(Outline in the possession of the author)

APPENDIX 8

....

OKW Directive No. 33 of 19 July 1941

1. The second series of battles in the east has ended along the entire front
   with the penetration of the Stalin Line and the further advance of the
   panzer groups. It will still require considerable time to eliminate the
   remaining enemy groups between the mobile formations of Army
   Group Centre.

   The northern wing of Army Group South is rendered immobile
   and ineffective by the Kiev fortress and by the Russian 5th Army in
   its rear.

2. The aim of the next operation must be to prevent the withdrawal of
   further strong enemy forces into the depths of Russia and to annihilate them. For this the following preparations will be made:

   (a) *Southern sector of the Eastern Front*

   The main objective is to destroy the enemy 12th and 6th Armies
   in a converging attack while they are still west of the Dnieper. . . .

   The enemy 5th Army can also be quickly and decisively crushed
   by cooperation between the forces on the southern wing of Army
   Group Centre and on the northern wing of Army Group South.
   Whilst the infantry divisions of Army Group Centre circle to the
   south, other forces, mainly mobile, after completing their current
   tasks, securing their supply lines, and providing cover against
   Moscow, will advance to the southeast, cutting off enemy forces
   on the opposite bank of the Dnieper from their escape deeper into

Russian territory and destroying them.

(b) *Central sector of the Eastern Front*

After eliminating several pockets of enemy troops and securing its supply lines, Army Group Centre, while continuing its advance on Moscow with infantry formations, will cut through the Moscow-Leningrad line with mobile units not already deployed to the southeast along the Dnieper, thereby covering the right flank of the advance by Army Group North on Leningrad.

(c) *Northern sector of the Eastern Front*

The advance on Leningrad is only to be resumed once the Eighteenth Army has made contact with Panzer Group 4 and once the eastern flank is reliably covered by the Sixteenth Army. Army Group North must endeavour to prevent Russian forces still fighting in Estonia from retreating to Leningrad. . . .

Items 3–5 relate to the Air Force, the Navy, and the western theatre of war.
(Nuremberg files, WFSt War Diary)

APPENDIX 9

....

*Organisation of the higher command and of
Panzer Group 3 on 21 June 1941*

ORGANISATION, DEPARTMENT, OR OFFICE	COMMANDING OFFICER
High Command of the Armed Forces (OKW)	Field-Marshal Wilhelm Keitel
Operations Staff of the Armed Forces (WFSt)	General of the Artillery Alfred Jodl
High Command of the Army (OKH)	Field-Marshal Walther von Brauchitsch
Chief of the General Staff of the Army	Colonel-General Franz Halder
Head Quartermaster I	Lieutenant-General Friedrich Paulus
Operations Section of the OKH	Colonel Adolf Heusinger
Army Group Centre	Field-Marshal Fedor von Bock
Chief of Staff of Army Group Centre	Major-General Hans von Greiffenberg
Ninth Army	Colonel-General Adolf Strauß
Panzer Group 3	Colonel-General Hermann Hoth (commander of the Seventeenth Army from 8 October 1941)
Chief of Staff of Panzer Group 3	Lieutenant-Colonel Walther von Hünersdorff
First General Staff Officer of Panzer Group 3	Major Carl Wagener
XXXIX Panzer Corps	General of Panzer Troops Rudolf Schmidt

Chief of Staff of the XXXIX Panzer Corps	Colonel Hans-Georg Hildebrandt
7th Panzer Division	Major-General Hans Freiherr von Funck
20th Panzer Division	Lieutenant-General Horst Stumpff
20th Motorised Infantry Division	Major-General Hans Zorn
14th Motorised Infantry Division	Major-General Friedrich Fürst
LVII Panzer Corps	General of Panzer Troops Adolf-Friedrich Kuntzen
Chief of Staff of the LVII Panzer Corps	Lieutenant-Colonel Friedrich Fangohr
12th Panzer Division	Major-General Josef Harpe
19th Panzer Division	Lieutenant-General Otto von Knobelsdorff
18th Infantry Division	Major-General Friedrich Herrlein
V Corps	General of the Infantry Richard Ruoff
Chief of Staff of the V Corps	Colonel Arthur Schmidt
5th Infantry Division	Major-General Karl Allmendinger
35th Infantry Division	Lieutenant-General Walther Fischer von Weikersthal
VI Corps	General of the Pioneers Otto-Wilhelm Förster
Chief of Staff of the VI Corps	Lieutenant-Colonel Hans Degen
6th Infantry Division	Lieutenant-General Helge Auleb
26th Infantry Division	Major-General Walter Weiss

In October the following formations were put under the command of Panzer Group 3

XLI Panzer Corps	General of Panzer Troops Georg-Hans Reinhardt
Chief of Staff of the XLI Panzer Corps	Colonel Hans Röttiger
1st Panzer Division	Major-General Walter Krüger
36th Infantry Division	Major-General Otto-Ernst Ottenbacher
LVI Panzer Corps	General of Panzer Troops Ferdinand Schaal
Chief of Staff of the LVI Panzer Corps	Colonel Harald Freiherr von Elverfeldt
6th Panzer Division	Major-General Franz Landgraf
7th Panzer Division	Major-General Hans Freiherr von Funck

High Command of the Seventeenth Army
Operations Section
No. 0973/41 (secret)

Army Command Post
17 November 1941

THE CONDUCT OF GERMAN SOLDIERS IN THE EAST

1. From observations during my trips to the front and from conversations with officers and enlisted personnel in the field, I have gained the impression that there exists no consistent understanding of our tasks in the conquered territory and therefore of the attitude to be taken by the soldiers.

    In the following I unequivocally reproduce the outlook, repeatedly expressed by the Führer, which must guide the entire armed forces. In the next few weeks it must be made the subject of discussions within the officer corps and must be conveyed to the troops.

PART I

2. The Eastern campaign must be conducted differently to the war against the French. During the summer it has become increasingly clear to us that two profoundly incompatible views have come into conflict here in the East. On the one side is a German sense of honour

and race, with centuries of military tradition. On the other are Asiatic doctrines and primitive instincts inflamed by a small number of mostly Jewish intellectuals: fear of the knout, contempt for moral values, descent into degradation, and disdain for lives deemed worthless.

More than ever we are occupied by the thought of a new era in which the German people shall reign supreme over Europe by virtue of their racial superiority and their accomplishments. We clearly recognise that our mission is to save European culture from the encroachment of Asiatic barbarism. We now know that we have to fight against a fierce and tenacious adversary. This fight can only end in the annihilation of one side or the other. There is no compromise.

3. This war has the following objectives:
    (a) To subjugate the Red Army such that it cannot recover.
    (b) To demonstrate to the Russian population the powerlessness of their former rulers and the inexorable will of the Germans to wipe out these rulers as bearers of Bolshevik thought.
    (c) To exploit conquered territory mercilessly so that army supply need not diminish home front supply.

PART II

4. After five months of continuous success, the military goal of this campaign has been reached. The colossal Soviet army is incapable of performing large-scale operations and of putting up coherent resistance. It was not to be expected that so great an empire would collapse in a single, short campaign over the summer and autumn. It is now imperative to mop up enemy industrial regions, which are of such importance for his armaments and overall economy. Moreover, everything must be done to prevent the enemy from rebuilding, even partially, his heavily shattered army over the winter.
5. Consequently, operations will not come to a complete standstill this winter. The Führer will not demand the impossible from the German soldiers. No German troops will be sacrificed in the Russian winter.

Appropriate measures will be taken in preparation for the particular conditions of warfare in the Russian winter. Furthermore, the time required for our troops to rest, for our units to be refitted, and for our supply to be secured will be given. But even during this pause in operations, some troops must be employed for defensive purposes and along our rear lines of communication. Contact with the enemy must be maintained through reconnaissance.

PART III: THE STRUGGLE AGAINST BOLSHEVISM

6. I expect every soldier of the Seventeenth Army to be proud of our achievements and to be filled with the feeling of absolute superiority. We are the masters of this land we have conquered. Our supremacy entails neither respite, nor negligence of our attitude and uniform, nor self-serving brutality, but rather conscious opposition to Bolshevism, strict military discipline, grim determination, and tireless vigilance.

7. Despite the pause in combat, the war is not over given that we still stand face to face with the Red adversary. He could not defeat us in open battle, but he intends to wear us down over the winter through guerrilla warfare. We must not allow him to succeed through carelessness and benevolence on our part, so we have to beware of anything accompanied by hostility or indifference! Anyone who fails to inform us of the activities of Red partisans is our enemy and will be treated accordingly. The fear of the population of our countermeasures is to be stronger than that of Stalinist intimidation.

8. Compassion towards the population is completely misguided. Red Army soldiers have brutally murdered our wounded comrades. They have harmed and killed prisoners. We like to think of how the population, which formerly endured the Bolshevik yoke, wants to win us over with kindness and servility. . . .

    The acquisition of food for the enemy population is to be left to local authorities. Any trace of active or passive resistance, or of any machinations by Jewish-Bolshevik agitators, is to be crushed immediately and mercilessly. The soldiers must understand clearly the necessity of harsh measures against elements alien to our nation and race. These elements are the spiritual pillars of Bolshevism, the representatives of murderous organisations, and the agents of partisans. They constitute the same Jewish subhumanity that has already caused great harm to our fatherland through hostility to our people and culture, that today promotes anti-German currents worldwide, and that wants to be the bearer of vengeance. Their annihilation is a requirement for self-preservation. Any soldier who criticises our measures forgets the years of destructive and treasonable activity against our own people by Jewish-Marxist elements.

PART IV: EXPLOITATION OF THE LAND

9. The natural wealth of the Ukraine has been heavily affected by the war. The enemy has removed or destroyed crops where he has had the opportunity to do so. Part of the harvest deteriorates in the fields. Requisitioning has greatly depleted cattle and horse stocks. Nevertheless, the occupied territory has to feed the entire German army, provide the seeds for cultivation, and avoid famine for the population.

10. Therefore, it must be clear to every man that the remaining stocks are not for individual access but for the general public. Any misappropriation harms the community. The full utilisation of the land is to be carried out systematically by the requisition parties of the divisions and corps. An officer may only order requisitioning if rations are undelivered. Requisitioned subsistence supplies are to be paid for. Anything else is 'plunder' and will be severely punished according to the laws of war.

11. It is the duty of every commander, even if he does not have the special task of preventing land stock of all kinds from being taken by individuals, to intervene immediately against plunder by individual soldiers and, if possible, to recover crops. We will draw extensively on the inhabitants for such recovery efforts. The population will be re-

quired, and if necessary forced, to help meet the supply demands of the German armed forces and of the German economy so as to ensure we reach our objectives. They shall work no less than the people of the German homeland. Every senior garrison officer has to monitor this. In the individual administrative districts, agricultural leaders are to be brought in from Germany. I ask that they be assisted in their work in every way.

PART V: THE OFFICER

12. The attitude of the officers and non-commissioned officers is crucial for that of the troops. The common man often thinks about the enemy more grimly and bitterly than the officer. The officer has to be prepared for this. A healthy sense of hatred and dislike for the situation must be strengthened rather than suppressed. But brutality, oppression, and cruelty are dishonourable. Never before throughout history has the German officer been in a more important position than in this war. It will be up to him to fulfill several tasks and to faultlessly endure the great exertions of the campaign in the coming winter. The more difficult the tasks are, the more focused the officer must be. His consistently positive, exemplary, and encouraging leadership shall overcome all timidity.

On a day-to-day basis we should not lose sight of the historical importance of our struggle against Soviet Russia. For the last two centuries Russia has had a paralysing effect on Europe. Consideration for Russia and concern for an invasion have always dominated the political situation in Europe and inhibited peaceful development. Russia is an Asiatic rather than a European state. Each step we take further into this enslaved and miserable country shows us this difference. We fight so as to forever liberate Europe, and especially Germany, from the pressure and destructive power of Bolshevism.

Signed by Hoth

APPENDIX 11

· ·

Hermann Hoth on the relief attack towards
Stalingrad and on responsibility

A: RELIEF ATTACK

The LVI Panzer Corps of the Fourth Panzer Army was to break through
in the direction of Stalingrad and establish contact with the encircled
Sixth Army. Parts of the Sixth Army were supposed to push towards us.

The Russians withdrew forces from combat against the Sixth Army and
threw them against us. After fierce fighting we reached a position approximately 50 kilometres away from the pocket. Here, we were
stopped by fresh enemy forces. For four days we did the utmost whilst
hoping for a counterattack by the Sixth Army. But the leadership of the
Sixth Army hesitated until it was too late.

Meanwhile, the situation west of the Don had become critical, so
Manstein had to send one of my divisions there. It became impossible
to continue our attack with the remaining forces. With heavy hearts we
had to withdraw the LVI Panzer Corps.

B: RESPONSIBILITY

For every military leader, whether a non-commissioned officer or a field
commander, responsibility is the heaviest, yet unavoidable, burden he

has to bear in war. He must be responsible for executing orders and for the soldiers under his command.

This responsibility cannot be taken off his shoulders, let alone from the highest commander. Since the time of Scharnhorst it has been the supreme law of Prussian-German leadership.

Responsibility has weighed heavily upon all those leading figures drawn into the disaster at Stalingrad, and they still carry this burden today. Their actions were guided by their conscience and by their awareness of their responsibility before God, not by responsibility to the dictator who threatened them with the loss of honour, freedom, and life.

(Document held by the Institut für Zeitgeschichte, Munich)

NOTES

....

1 Carl von Clausewitz discusses the terms 'strategy' and 'tactics' in *Vom Kriege*, book 2, chapter 1.

2 Clausewitz, book 2, chapter 1, p. 169.

3 *Ibid.*

4 Clausewitz, book 8, chapter 6, p. 891.

5 Erich von Manstein, *Verlorene Siege*, Bonn: Athenäum-Verlag, 1952, p. 153ff.

6 In his brilliant study, 'Operationen' (*Wehrwissenschaftliche Rundschau*, vol. 3, p. 1), General Georg von Sodenstern counted deployment as strategy because the deployment orders are independent of the will of the enemy, whilst in operations 'our will shall very soon encounter the will of the enemy' (Moltke).

7 Refer to Rudolf Stadelmann, *Moltke und der Staat*, Krefeld: Scherz-Verlag, 1950, for further details about the apolitical Moltke the elder and his politically minded successor Alfred Graf von Waldersee.

8 In one of his studies shortly before the Second World War, Colonel-General Beck warned against the 'belief in the omnipotence of operations' (Ludwig Beck, *Studien*, edited by Hans Speidel, Stuttgart: K. F. Koehler, 1955, p. 85), and was sceptical of the possibility of accelerating offensive actions through the use of tanks (Beck, p. 59).

9 J. F. C. Fuller, 'Der Krieg und die Zukunft', *Wehrwissenschaftliche Rundschau* (1953).

10 Details in Herbert von Borsch, 'Politische Paradoxien des Atomzeitalters', *Außenpolitik*, issue 7 (1951).

11 The book by George Cooper Reinhardt and William Roscoe Kintner (*Atomwaffen im Landkrieg*, Darmstadt: Wehr- und Wissen-Verlag-Gesellschaft, 1955) provides detailed information about the effects of nuclear weapons and the means of protection against them.

12 Field-Marshal Montgomery commented during a command-post exercise he led in April 1956 that 'we are entering the era of guided missiles'. See *Wehrkunde*, issue 8 (1956).

13 Clausewitz in an essay of 1804, *Strategie*, ed. Eberhard Kessel, Hanseatische Verlagsanstalt.

14 Clausewitz, book 2, chapter 6, p. 237.

15 Scharnhorst, 'Nutzen der militärischen Geschichte', cited in Reinhard Höhn, *Scharnhorsts Vermächtnis*, Bonn: Athenäum-Verlag, 1952, p. 70.

16 Scharnhorst, 'Bruchstücke über Erfahrung und Theorie', cited in Rudolf Stadelmann, *Scharnhorst: Schicksal und geistige Welt*, Wiesbaden: Limes-Verlag, 1952, p. 155ff.

17 For example in Manstein, p. 152ff. Also in Kurt von Tippelskirch, *Geschichte des zweiten Weltkrieges*, Bonn: Athenäum-Verlag, 1951, pp. 198, 209, as well as in Kurt Assmann, *Deutsche Schicksalsjahre*, Wiesbaden: Brockhaus, 1951.

18 Gerhard L. Weinberg, 'Der deutsche Entschluß zum Angriff auf die Sowjetunion', *Vierteljahreshefte für Zeitgeschichte*, vol. 1, issue 4 (1953).

19 Documents for the Nuremberg Trials 1946-48, Halder's diary, 26 July 1940.

20 Halder's diary, 27 July 1940.

21 Weinberg.

22 Halder's diary, 31 July 1940, 1 August 1940, and 29 October 1940.

23 Alfred Philippi, 'Das Pripjetproblem', *Wehrwissenschaftliche Rundschau*, supplement no. 2 (March 1956). This insightful study, which mainly deals with the operations of Army Group South, publishes an excerpt from the so-called 'Marcks Plan' and refutes the opinion given in foreign works (e.g. J. F. C. Fuller, *The Second World War: A Strategical and Tactical History*, London: Eyre & Spottiswoode, 1948) that General Marcks advocated 'offense with all available forces south of the Pripet Marshes over the Dnieper to Rostov-on-Don' and 'defence between Pinsk and Riga'. Unfortunately, details of the study concerning Army Group Centre cannot be covered here.

24 Halder's diary, 31 July 1940, 1 August 1940, and 29 October 1940.

25 *Ibid.*

26 Helmuth Greiner, *Die oberste Wehrmachtführung 1939-1943*, Wiesbaden: Limes-Verlag, 1951, p. 308.

27 OKH War Diary, vol. 6a.

28 *Ibid.*

29 Greiner, p. 330.

30 OKH War Diary, vol. 1.

31 Heinz Guderian, *Erinnerungen eines Soldaten*, Heidelberg: K. Vowinckel, 1951, appendix 21. Guderian has not been subjected to a military tribunal investigation.

32 Helmuth Karl Bernhard von Moltke, *Militärische Werke: Kriegslehren*, Berlin: Mittler und Sohn, 1911, part 1, p. 72.

33 Documents for the Nuremberg Trials 1946-48, Studie Hitlers, 22 August 1941, on the general conduct of the war against Russia.

34 Clausewitz, book 8, chapter 9, p. 922.

35 Halder's diary, 17 August 1941. On this day Halder confided to his notebook the realisation 'that Russia had been underestimated'.

36 Documents for the Nuremberg Trials 1946–48, in OKW 2705, 'Deployment Orders for Barbarossa'.

37 OKW War Diary, vol. 44.

38 Tippelskirch, pp. 201, 229.

39 Manstein, p. 305.

40 See Deployment Orders for Panzer Group 3, Appendix 1.

41 See also Guderian, p. 136. The deployment orders mentioned here are those of the OKH, which Panzer Group 2 also did not receive.

42 War Diary of Army Group North, 19 March 1941. Halder in a long-distance call with the first general staff officer of Army Group North, Lieutenant-Colonel Paul Reinhold Herrmann: 'The commander of Army Group North [Field-Marshal Wilhelm Ritter von Leeb] wanted to put strong infantry forces under the command of Panzer Group 4. This measure was rejected as highly inexpedient by the commander of the panzer group [Hoepner] on the basis of his experience in the Western campaign' (Documents for the Nuremberg Trials 1946-48, in OKW 1653). See also Guderian, p. 132.

43 Moltke, part 1, p. 70.

44 Moltke, part 1, p. 71.

45 Halder's diary, 24 and 25 June 1941.

46 Halder's diary, 30 June 1941.

47 Guderian, pp. 139-44.

48 Manstein, pp. 181-5.

49 Georg-Hans Reinhardt, 'Der Vorstoß des XXXXI. Panzerkorps im Sommer 1941', Wehrkunde, issue 3 (1956).

50 Moltke, part 1, p. 71.

51 Ibid.

52 Documents for the Nuremberg Trials 1946-48, P.S. 1799, special records, appendix 6.

53 Documents for the Nuremberg Trials 1946-48, OKW, special records, 27 and 29 June 1941.

54 Documents for the Nuremberg Trials 1946-48, OKW/L, War Diary, vol. 8.

55 Documents for the Nuremberg Trials 1946-48, memorandum by Hitler, 21 August 1941.

56 Halder's diary, 1-2 July 1941.

57 Otto von Knobelsdorff, *Geschichte der 19. Panzer-Division*, unpublished manuscript.

58 Guderian, pp. 146-7.

59 Manstein, pp. 186-7; Reinhardt, 'Der Vorstoß des XXXXI. Panzerkorps'.

60 Kluge's Fourth Panzer Army existed only in July 1941. It is distinct from the 'second' Fourth Panzer Army, which from January 1942 was a redesignated Panzer Group 4. Guderian, p. 150, surmised that Panzer Groups 2 and 3 were subordinated to Kluge at Bock's request 'so that he would be unburdened from direct responsibility for their leadership'. There is no confirmation of this in the documents. Even on 24 June 1941 Halder had considered uniting both panzer groups under the command of Kluge or Guderian (Halder's diary, 24 June 1941). The subordination to Kluge occurred despite Guderian's threat to resign his command. See Halder's diary, 10 July 1941.

61 Documents for the Nuremberg Trials 1946-48, in OKW/L, volume 8.

62 Halder's diary, 3 July 1941.

63 As reported by Army Group Centre (Halder's diary, 9 July 1941).

64 Knobelsdorff.

65 Halder's diary, 9 July 1941. Guderian does not mention any written order from the Fourth Panzer Army.

66 Guderian, pp. 152–3.

67 Halder's diary, 10 July 1941.

68 Halder's diary, 9 July 1941.

69 Order of Panzer Group 3, section 2, on 3 July 1941, in the possession of the author.

70 Documents for the Nuremberg Trials 1946-48, P.S., appendix 11.

71 The 'Stalin Line' was the designation invented by the propaganda ministry for a series of unrelated permanent fortifications on the former Russian western frontier, e.g. northwest of Minsk against Poland, south of Pskov against Estonia, and in other places.

72 Documents for the Nuremberg Trials 1946-48, OKW special records and Halder's diary, 8 July 1941.

73 Intelligence Report No. 18 of Panzer Group 3 on 8 July 1941, in the possession of the author.

74 From notes in the possession of the author.

75 Knobelsdorff.

76 Order of Panzer Group 3, section 2, on 3 July 1941, in the possession of the author.

77 Guderian, p. 162.

78 Guderian, pp. 160-4, suggests that he would have liked to provide the assistance needed by Panzer Group 3 for the encirclement of the Russians in and to the north of Smolensk, but because of insufficient forces was unable to do so. This is not entirely true. The encirclement was the joint task of both panzer groups: Panzer Group 2 to the south and Panzer Group 3 to the north of the highway. Since 15 July the latter stood on the highway west of Yartsevo and waited there in vain for contact with Panzer Group 2. Neither the 17th nor the 18th Panzer Divisions received appropriate orders after being freed from the west of Smolensk. The 17th Panzer Division was committed to a security mission on the Dnieper, approximately 50 kilometres south of Yartsevo (Guderian, p. 163), and the 18th Panzer Division was moved to Pochinok, 50 kilometres south of Smolensk, in order to 'protect an advance landing field against bombardment by Russian artillery and mortars' (Guderian, p. 164). Clear orders from the Fourth Panzer Army were obviously lacking.

79 Halder's diary, 12 July 1941.

80 Halder's diary, 13 July 1941.

81 *Ibid.*

82 Knobbeldorff.

83 Combat report of Panzer Group 3 in Russia.

84 Reinhardt, 'Der Vorstoß des XXXXI. Panzerkorps', p. 135.

85 *Ibid.*, p. 129.

86 Erhard Raus, 'Im Tor nach Leningrad', *Wehrwissenschaftliche Rundschau*, issue 3 (March 1953).

87 Manstein, pp. 195–7.

88 Raus, 'Im Tor nach Leningrad'.

89 Nuremberg documents, in OKW/L, War Diary, vol. 8.

90 Nuremberg documents, PS 1799, special records, appendix 18.

91 Nuremberg documents, memorandum by Hitler, 21 August 1941.

92 Nuremberg documents, OKH directive on 28 July 1941, OKW War Diary, vol. 8.

93 Halder's diary, 21 July 1941.

94 Halder's diary, 19 July 1941.

95 Halder to the then Head Quartermaster I, Major-General Paulus (Halder's diary, 26 July 1941).

96 Meeting between Brauchitsch and Hitler on 23 July 1941 (Nuremberg documents, OKW War Diary, vol. 8).

97 Clausewitz, book 8, chapter 9, p. 919.

98 Nuremberg documents, P.S. 1799, Chief of the OKW, No. 1419, 54/41.

99 Nuremberg documents, OKW War Diary, vol. 8.

100 Nuremberg documents, OKH, Operations Section, War Diary, part C, vol. 2.

101 Nuremberg documents, appendix to OKH, Operations Section, 1401/41, 28 July 1941.

102 Nuremberg documents, P.S. 1799, special records, appendix 23.

103 Nuremberg documents, P.S. 1799, special records, appendix 24.

104 *Armeegruppe Guderian* (Army Group Guderian), not to be confused with a full army group, e.g. *Heeresgruppe Mitte* (Army Group Centre).

105 Nuremberg documents, P.S. 1799, special records, appendix 25.

106 Nuremberg documents, OKH directive on 28 July 1941, Chief of Staff of the Army, operations section, 1440/41.

107 Nuremberg documents, WFSt War Diary, appendix 13.

108 Halder's diary, 5 August 1941.

109 Halder's diary, 7 August 1941.

110 Guderian, p. 171; Halder's diary, 4 August 1941.

111 Guderian, pp. 176-8.

112 Hans Steets, *Gebirgsjäger bei Uman: Die Korpsschlacht des XXXXIX. Gebirgs-Armeekorps bei Podwyssokoje 1941*, Heidelberg: Scharnhorst Buchkameradenschaft, 1955.

113 Reinhardt, 'Der Vorstoß des XXXXI. Panzerkorps', p. 131.

114 Nuremberg documents, P.S. 1799, special records, appendix 32, OKW/L, War Diary.

115 Nuremberg documents, WFSt War Diary, appendix 9.

116 Halder's diary, 3 August 1941.

117 Nuremberg documents, P.S. 1799, special records, appendix 36, OKW No. 941386, 15 August 1941.

118 Manstein, p. 201.

119 Manstein, p. 203.

120 Knobelsdorff.

121 Nuremberg documents, OKH Chief of Staff, Barbarossa III.

122 Nuremberg documents, P.S. 1799, WFSt/L 441412/41.

123 Clausewitz, 'Die wichtigsten Grundsätze des Kriegführens usw'., p. 978.

124 Moltke, p. 71, footnote.

125 Georg-Hans Reinhardt, 'Panzer-Gruppe 3 in der Schlacht von Moskau', *Wehrkunde*, issue 9 (1953).

126 Guderian, p. 213.

127 Clausewitz, book 8, chapter 9.

128 Further details in Dr Ferdinand Maria von Senger und Etterlin, 'Der Marsch einer Panzerdivision in der Schlammperiode', *Wehrkunde*, issue 3 (1955).

129 Quoted from Stadelmann, *Scharnhorst*, p. 165.

130 See appendix 2 for the directive for the conduct of operations by Panzer Group 3.

131 Barbarossa Day.

132 Translator's note: Though not present in the German edition, this order by Hoth from 17 November 1941 is included in this translation because it provides insight into his view of the ideological nature of the war on the Eastern Front. Likewise, Appendix 11 has been added to this edition for its insight into Hoth's thinking after he had participated in the German disaster at Stalingrad.

BIBLIOGRAPHY

Published works

Allgemeine Schweizerische Militärzeitschrift

Assmann, Kurt, *Deutsche Schicksalsjahre*, Wiesbaden: Brockhaus, 1951

Beck, Ludwig, *Studien*, edited by Hans Speidel, Stuttgart: K. F. Koehler, 1955

Borsch, Herbert von, 'Politische Paradoxien des Atomzeitalters', *Außen-politik*, issue 7 (1951)

Clausewitz, Carl von, *Strategie aus dem Jahr 1804, mit Zusätzen von 1808 und 1809*, Hamburg: Hanseatische Verlagsanstalt, 1937

Clausewitz, Carl von, *Vom Kriege*, 16th edition, Bonn: Dümmlers Verlag, 1952 [in English: *On War*, trans. Michael Howard & Peter Paret, Princeton: Princeton University Press, 1976 (revised 1984)]

Fuller, J. F. C., 'Der Krieg und die Zukunft', *Wehrwissenschaftliche Rund-schau* (1953)

Fuller, J. F. C., *The Second World War: A Strategical and Tactical History*, London: Eyre & Spottiswoode, 1948

Greiner, Helmuth, *Die oberste Wehrmachtführung 1939–1943*, Wiesbaden: Limes-Verlag, 1951

Guderian, Heinz, *Erinnerungen eines Soldaten*, Heidelberg: K. Vowinckel, 1951 [in English: *Panzer Leader*, trans. Constantine Fitzgibbon, London: Michael Joseph, 1952]

Höhn, Reinhard, *Scharnhorsts Vermächtnis*, Bonn: Athenäum-Verlag, 1952

Manstein, Erich von, *Verlorene Siege*, Bonn: Athenäum-Verlag, 1955 [in

English: *Lost Victories*, trans. Anthony G. Powell, London: Methuen, 1958]

Moltke, Helmuth Karl Bernhard von, *Militärische Werke: Kriegslehren*, Berlin: Mittler und Sohn, 1911

Philippi, Alfred, 'Das Pripjetproblem', *Wehrwissenschaftliche Rundschau*, supplement no. 2 (March 1956)

Erhard Raus, 'Im Tor nach Leningrad', *Wehrwissenschaftliche Rundschau*, issue 3 (March 1953)

Reinhardt, George Cooper & Kintner, William Roscoe, *Atomwaffen im Landkrieg*, Darmstadt: Wehr- und Wissen-Verlag-Gesellschaft, 1955 [in English: *Atomic Weapons in Land Combat*, Harrisburg, PA: Military Service Pub. Co., 1954]

Reinhardt, Georg-Hans, 'Der Vorstoß des XXXXI. Panzerkorps im Sommer 1941', *Wehrkunde*, issue 3 (1956)

Reinhardt, Georg-Hans, 'Panzer-Gruppe 3 in der Schlacht von Moskau', *Wehrkunde*, issue 9 (1953)

Senger und Etterlin, Dr Ferdinand Maria von, 'Der Marsch einer Panzerdivision in der Schlammperiode', *Wehrkunde*, issue 3 (1955)

Sodenstern, Georg von, 'Operationen', *Wehrwissenschaftliche Rundschau*, vol. 3

Stadelmann, Rudolf, *Moltke und der Staat*, Krefeld: Scherz-Verlag, 1950

Stadelmann, Rudolf, *Scharnhorst: Schicksal und geistige Welt*, Wiesbaden: Limes-Verlag, 1952

Steets, Hans, *Gebirgsjäger bei Uman: Die Korpsschlacht des XXXXIX. Gebirgs-Armeekorps bei Podwyssokoje 1941*, Heidelberg: Scharnhorst Buchkameradenschaft, 1955

Tippelskirch, Kurt von, *Geschichte des zweiten Weltkrieges*, Bonn: Athenäum-Verlag, 1951

Wehrkunde, issue 8 (1956)

Weinberg, Gerhard L., 'Der deutsche Entschluß zum Angriff auf die Sowjetunion', *Vierteljahreshefte für Zeitgeschichte*, vol. 1, issue 4 (1953)

Unpublished manuscripts

Combat report of Panzer Group 3 in Russia, 10 February 1942
Documents for the Nuremberg Trials 1946–48, including:
    Halder's Diary
    War Diaries
Knobelsdorff, Otto von, *Geschichte der 19. Panzer-Division*
Progress in combat by Panzer Group 4